SIX PILLARS FROM EPHESIANS

*Life
Overflowing*

# T.D. JAKES

## SIX PILLARS FROM EPHESIANS

# *Life Overflowing*

## THE SPIRITUAL WALK OF THE BELIEVER

BETHANYHOUSE

MINNEAPOLIS, MINNESOTA

*Six Pillars From Ephesians: Life Overflowing*
*The Spiritual Walk of the Believer*
Copyright © 2000 by T. D. Jakes
T. D. Jakes Ministries

Unless otherwise indicated, all Scripture quotations are taken from the *King James Version* of the Holy Bible.

Scripture quotations marked NIV are taken from the *Holy Bible, New International Version.*® NIV®. Copyright © 1973, 1978, 1984 by International Bible Society. Used by permission of Zondervan Publishing House. All right reserved.

Scripture quotations identified NKJV are from the *New King James Version* of the Bible. Copyright © 1979, 1980, 1982 by Thomas Nelson, Inc. Used by permission. All rights reserved.

Published by Bethany House Publishers
11400 Hampshire Avenue South
Bloomington, Minnesota 55438
www.bethanyhouse.com
Bethany House Publishers is a Division of Baker Book House Company, Grand Rapids, Michigan.

Printed in the United States of America.

---

**Library of Congress Cataloging-in-Publication Data**

Jakes, T. D.
      Life overflowing : the spiritual walk of the believer / by T. D. Jakes.
            p.   cm.– (Six pillars from Ephesians ; v. 4)
Originally published: Tulsa, Okla. : Albury Pub., c2000. (Jakes, T. D. Six pillars from Ephesians ; v. 4) Includes bibliographical references.
      ISBN 0-7642-2842-0 (pbk.)
      1. Christian life–Biblical teaching.  2. Bible. N.T. Ephesians –Criticism, interpretation, etc.  I. Title  II. Series: Jakes, T. D. Six pillars from Ephesians ; v. 4.
      BS2695.6.C48J35 2003
      248'.4–dc22                                          2003014740

# CONTENTS

# LIFE OVERFLOWING
# THE SPIRITUAL WALK
# OF THE BELIEVER

**I N T R O D U C T I O N**

The book of Ephesians reveals to us the mystery, the majesty, and the beauty of the Church. In the beginning, the apostle Paul arrests our attention with the Holy Spirit's description of who we are and what we can and should do as the Bride of Christ. In the end, we are overwhelmed and blessed to be a part of such an exquisite union, yet intensely sober as Paul drills into us our responsibility to protect the reputation of Jesus Christ in our walk with Him.

The apostle Paul is an interesting personality in the kingdom of God. Credited with writing approximately two-thirds of the New Testament, he is best known for his unshakable zeal for God. His intense allegiance to the will of God is awe-inspiring, but embedded in all of his teaching is his passion for developing and maturing believers. His mission in life is to prepare us to represent Jesus Christ in the earth. It is not enough for us to enjoy our salvation; we must also appreciate and respect the responsibilities associated with it.

Our actions, lifestyle, and the manner in which we relate to people are of paramount importance to Paul. He demands that we "walk worthy of the vocation [calling] wherewith ye are called" (Ephesians 4:1). In other words, we should conduct our lives in such a way that the Lord would not regret having saved us. At this challenge, many questions arise:

How willing are we to accept the responsibility of our actions?

How committed are we to protecting the reputation of God?

Are we genuinely walking with the Lord, or are we stumbling through this life?

Our walk with Christ is not a stroll around the block — it is a power walk! We do not walk in our own strength or wisdom, but in the power of the Holy Spirit, who speaks only of Jesus, continually revealing His goodness, His justice, and His grace. Thus, we walk with integrity, because we feel responsible to represent Him well. The way we choose our steps demonstrates to all who watch us that we walk with divine, inspired purpose. He died for us, He called us, He loves us — and we will not let Him down.

We walk with an erect posture, looking toward our future. We are not wandering aimlessly as though we have no place to go and nothing to do. He has called us out of our dull and sinful lives into the glorious kingdom of God to fulfill His purpose and plan for our lives.

Jesus saved us, and in so doing He gave us a new nature. Now we are new creatures in Christ. Old things passed away the day we were convicted, convinced, and converted. And so we walk in dignity, strength, and — most of all — love. Energized by His Spirit, motivated by His love, and guided by His wisdom, we walk into *Life Overflowing*.

Prepare yourself now to discover the joy of power-walking with God. Don't forget your stretching exercises of prayer and faith! Be sure to wear some comfortable shoes, because you are about to negotiate your way through rocky terrain. And there's no need to be afraid, because it is not your walk or my walk — but our walk with God. Now, let's get started!

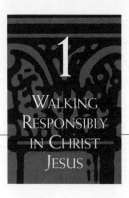

The Church represents Jesus to the world. We are the *body* of Christ, which means we are Jesus Christ's physical presence in the earth today. But what is our specific responsibility to God as His individual children? Paul brings us right to that point in the first verse of the fourth chapter of Ephesians:

> **A**s a prisoner for the Lord, then, I urge you to live a life worthy of the calling you have received.
>
> EPHESIANS 4:1 NIV

How many books are on the market today telling people how to set goals and reach them? How many people are giving talks about how to dream big dreams and fulfill them? How many plans are there for mapping out the future and achieving great things? They are beyond counting! Yet, most of those books, talks, and plans are based upon man's ability to set his own agenda, map out his own life, determine his own goals, and then reach those goals on his own effort, using his own intelligence and skills and exerting his own strength and power. That's *not* what God has for the believer! The believer is to walk out *God's plan.*

## WALKING OUT GOD'S PLAN

The Holy Spirit is not committed to any plans other than those of God the Father and of the Son, Jesus Christ. We are dead wrong before God when we come to Him and say, "Here's my idea. I'm asking You to put Your stamp on it and help me do it." No!

**F**or we are his workmanship, created in Christ Jesus unto good works, which God hath before ordained that we should walk in them.

EPHESIANS 2:10

Our position must always be, "Lord, show me Your plan. Teach me the way I am to walk. Give me Your instructions." And then when we know with certainty in our hearts and minds what God desires for us to do, we are to do the walking. He isn't going to walk for us; rather, He empowers us *as we walk in Him.* He helps us, encourages us, counsels us, and comforts us with His presence.

The Lord is committed to His plans and purposes, and only to His plans and purposes. He is committed to us always in His love, but He is committed to the fulfillment of our plans and purposes only if they are in alignment with His. We are called by God to walk in a very specific way and in a specific direction. In essence, that is our calling. We don't just walk around aimlessly in this life; our walk accomplishes God's plans and purposes, which is our calling. Some believers seem to think that only pastors, evangelists, or missionaries are called by God; but the fact is, every believer is called.

> **A**s a prisoner for the Lord, then, I urge you to live a life worthy of the calling you have received.
>
> EPHESIANS 4:1 NIV

The phrase "prisoner for the Lord" is *desmios en kurio* in the Greek. This phrase is more than a statement of fact. *Desmios* means "prisoner" and refers to the actual state of confinement Paul endured. However, Paul calls this incarceration "prisoner for the Lord." You would expect him to say, "prisoner *of* the Lord." The word "for" signifies that from Paul's perspective, he was not a captive of Nero, but of Jesus.

There is a metaphorical meaning to the word "prisoner" here as well. It can mean "binding as with a spell." Paul is captivated by Jesus Christ and counts his imprisonment as nothing more than a symbol of his position in Him. Therefore, Paul cherishes and glories in his confinement. Theodoret put it this way: "He glories in his chains more than a king glories in his crown."

When Paul wrote this, he was under house arrest in Rome, but he didn't regard himself as a prisoner of the Romans. He was a prisoner of Jesus Christ — a voluntary slave — totally in subjection to Jesus. He goes where Jesus tells him to go, he endures what Jesus puts before him to endure, he walks where Jesus tells him to walk, he says what Jesus tells him to say. He is *completely committed* to Jesus' call on his life.

Through the years, Paul's commitment brought him to a level of intimacy with the Lord. It began on the road to Damascus, when he was extraordinarily beckoned to the service of God and arrested by a blinding light. He was summarily repudiated by believers, which only strengthened his resolve to pursue his Lord. Thus he was driven into the Arabian desert to be forever yoked with the Lord.

After years of intense study and infusion of divine truth at the foot of Jesus, Paul bursts into the church at Jerusalem and confronts them with kingdom principles. He risks relationship with the apostles to champion the true Gospel — that where the Spirit of the Lord is, there is liberty. The Church is to walk in the freedom of the Spirit and is no longer in bondage to the rules of religion.

Paul pays a severe price for his submission to the will of God and ultimately bears in his body the marks of Christ Jesus. By the time he writes to the Ephesians, he is seasoned, tempered, and has been refined like gold. All of his trials and experiences have brought him to compel the Ephesians to walk worthy of their calling, to be completely committed and fully submitted to Jesus in every area of their lives.

The call of God is ever before us, driving us to the place God desires us to go and propelling us into the position where we will fulfill His purpose for our lives. Every believer has a call on their lives. Some are called to preach; others are called to establish businesses. But no matter the particular assignment, we all contribute to God's grand design for the kingdom.

## THE CALL SHATTERS LIMITATIONS

The call of God is continuously tugging on our hearts to go forward, propelling us to the next level of what God has for us. We cannot say that we have attained, but rather that we pursue the call of God. It is a haunting, nagging feeling that extends itself ahead of us and motivates us to move forward. A true call of God is always beyond our grasp. It is what causes us to grow, to excel, to seek — to extend ourselves beyond ourselves. And it is in this impossible place that we are humbled, knowing that we are being assigned a task which exceeds our ability.

God's call resonates in our potential, not in our present reality or natural capability. He never stops calling us to take one more step, do one more thing, engage in one more act of our faith. We are always in a position to *pursue* the call of God. As we reach to attain that calling, we excel and are humbled at the same time. We are perpetually in a position where we must become more like Jesus in order to succeed. Thus, the pursuit of excellence and humility of spirit co-exist as we walk in our calling.

Years ago I preached that God never asks a person to do something they can't do. The more I studied God's Word, however, the more I realized that God often asks people to do things they cannot do. He asked Peter to walk on water. He asked the lame man to take up his bed and walk. He asked dead Lazarus to come out of the grave. The very essence of God's calling on us is to challenge us to do something that is humanly impossible.

What God does is this: He endows us with His rich grace so that we might attain those things that are beyond our human comprehension or effort. When we say yes to His call and move in obedience and faith, He imparts the ability we lack to perform His will. The Lord does not impart His ability first and then call to us. He calls to us, and *as we step out in faith and obedience,* He imparts His ability.

The challenge each of us faces is to walk as if we have already arrived at the point to which God is calling us. We must first understand who we are in the body, what God has in His plan for us, and then *walk as if we were there.* Our walk should be a divine reflection of our calling. We should be able to look at our walk — its worthiness, preparation, and influence — and be able to recognize our calling. In other words, our walk will reflect our call.

I saw a television program about poor students who were attending an excellent high school in which the teachers and principals believed in them, held high goals for them, and challenged them to excellence. One of the students said, "When I come here, it's as if I'm coming to work. I have a job to do, and my job is to graduate from this school with the best grades possible, to get a scholarship, to go to college, to make something of myself, and to change this community for the better." That student spoke with conviction. Her head was held high. She had a gleam in her eye, a strength to her being. She was already walking in her future! She was walking as if she had already achieved all that was put before her.

Like this student, we must operate in God's vision for us. We must walk according to the portrait He has painted of our future. More than that, each of us must know that to fulfill God's plan, our lives must epitomize our call. The splendor of God's call must be reflected by our steadfast faith and obedience.

## THE POWER OF WALKING "IN SYNC"

> **A**s a prisoner for the Lord, then, I urge you to live a life worthy of the calling you have received.
>
> EPHESIANS 4:1 NIV

The word "walk" in Ephesians 4:1 does not refer to some sort of meandering stroll. It means to walk in a synchronized way, with the same rhythm and pattern. It means to walk in step with the Lord, to catch the beat of the Holy Spirit, and to move precisely as He moves. When God acts, we act. When God pauses, we pause.

We must never think we can compartmentalize our life to the point where we say, "In this category, in this season, in this circumstance, I am operating on my own. In this other category, other season, and other circumstance, I am operating according to the power of the Holy Spirit in me." The Holy Spirit does not come and go from our lives. He is always in us.

Our entire life, our entire walk is in Christ. As Paul preached to a crowd in Athens, "In him we live, and move, and have our being" (Acts 17:28). Every step of our walk, every day, must be synchronized with the Holy Spirit.

Now, to walk to the beat of the Holy Spirit means that you will *not* be walking to the beat of the world! What you hear in your spirit will be different than what you hear with your ears all around you. Unfortunately, some believers are so enthralled and impressed by the world, they never get quiet enough to hear the soft steady beat of the Holy Spirit inside them. As a result, they miss all God has for them.

Let me assure you of this, once you begin to walk to the rhythm of the Holy Spirit, nothing is going to matter as much to you as keeping pace with Him. You will find that the direction He moves is always the right direction. His timing is always the right timing, and the results are always the best results.

The Holy Spirit challenges us, inspires us, empowers us, helps us, and causes our efforts to be effective. He works through us as we engage our minds, open our mouths, move our feet, and use our hands according to His will. Most of us have not begun to move into the fullness of all that the Holy Spirit has prepared for us, however, and the apostle Paul is continually challenging us to do so.

> **A**nd to know the love of Christ, which passeth knowledge, that ye might be filled with all the fulness of God.
> Now unto him that is able to do exceeding abundantly above all that we ask or think, according to the power that worketh in us,
> Unto him be glory in the church by Christ Jesus throughout all ages, world without end. Amen.
>
> EPHESIANS 3:19-21

This passage of Scripture is the last part of Paul's prayer for the Ephesian believers in chapter three, and it prefaces his call to walk worthy of our calling in Ephesians 4:1. These verses are so rich, we must consider them in more detail. Paul begins by praying that the believers would become intimately aware of the love of Christ. He is convinced that a believer's excitement about the work of the kingdom is in direct proportion to their working knowledge of how much Jesus loves them.

Paul characterizes Jesus' love as "passing knowledge" love. What he is saying is that the love of Jesus for us is a love that cannot be fully understood.

18

The Greek word for "passing" is *huperballo*. It is a  compound word with two parts: *huper* and *ballo*. *Huper* means "to exceed or go beyond." *Ballo* means "to throw." In other words, the love of Jesus exceeds the goal. Whatever our need for love is, Jesus' love for us goes far beyond that requirement.

Some people might take exception to the concept of anything that is so great, it cannot be fully known (passing knowledge). However, Paul is not indicting the believer's ability to discover the love of Jesus. Rather, he is describing the expansive dimensions of that love and declaring that even if a lifetime is devoted to the pursuit of this knowledge, life would end before the task was complete. Clearly, then, Jesus Christ has so great a love for us, we cannot conceive of its height, width, or depth.

In Ephesians 3:20, Paul brings his prayer to its natural conclusion. If Jesus has so much love for us that we cannot fully comprehend it, then what kind of help can we expect to receive from Him? Paul's answer is that the help Jesus provides for the believer is "exceeding abundantly." Most literary people would frown on Paul's use of both "exceeding" and "abundantly," but both of these words together are still not sufficient to express Paul's original thought.

"Exceeding abundantly" in the English text represents one word in the original Greek text. That word is literally translated "quite beyond all measure." But even this expression is not enough for Paul. He further defines the quality of Jesus' help by stating that what the Lord will do for His loved ones is too great to "imagine." Literally, he challenges the believer to prescribe their own deliverance, spend quality time making sure that they have covered all the bases, crossed all the "t's," and dotted all the "i's." Then, when you have come up with a plan, formula, and strategy, you will still fall short of anticipating how great Jesus' deliverance will be for you.

The Lord says to His people, "I love you with a love that passes your ability to comprehend it. I believe in you far more than you believe in yourself. I have unfathomable riches in glory for you. I am come that you might have life, and that you might have it more abundantly." (See John 10:10.)

Everything the Lord does, He does in abundance, an overflowing outworking to facilitate and enable us to fulfill our purpose, our walk. And when it comes to our walk, it is also far bigger, far greater, and far more awesome than most of us recognize, believe, or can even imagine.

What we each must do, of course, is to train our ears to respond only to the call of God and to react only according to the beat of the Holy Spirit. Paul gives us instruction about how to do this in the next verses. He says,

> **W**alk with all lowliness and meekness, with long-suffering, forbearing one another in love,
> Endeavoring to keep the unity of the Spirit in the bond of peace.
>
> EPHESIANS 4:2-3 NKJV

We cannot step out in faith and obedience to fulfill an impossible calling without understanding the unfathomable love God has for us, that He will not fail us in any way or leave us stranded in our own ability. And then, as we walk according to His call on our lives, our lives are intertwined with one another and He calls us to love one another as He has loved us. "Forbearing one another in love" is one of the keys to our being able to fulfill our calling, and we accomplish this through an attitude of lowliness and meekness.

## LOWLINESS AND MEEKNESS

The call of God is always a high calling. We must never think of God's call as a call to a low position of authority, strength, or spiritual power. God's call is a calling that challenges us to go from strength to strength and from glory to glory. It is a calling to move up the mountain to ever greater heights. But the paradox of God is this: The higher the calling, the lower we must become in our own eyes. Jesus said about John the Baptist, "Among those that are born of women there is not a greater prophet" (Luke 7:28). John the Baptist, however, said of Jesus and his relationship to Him, "He must increase, but I must decrease" (John 3:30).

The apostle Paul had one of the greatest callings this world has ever known. He contributed more to the New Testament than any other apostle. Without his epistles, we would know far less about how the Church is to function. We would have far less understanding about the mystery of our faith in Christ Jesus. Yet Paul said of himself, "Christ Jesus came into the world to save sinners; of whom I am chief" (1 Timothy 1:15).

If you believe God has called you to greatness, your response to that call should be to fall on your face. As best I can tell, every great man and woman of God responded to God's call on their lives by falling prostrate on the floor before the Lord. When an angel of the Lord appeared to Zacharias and told him he would have a son named John, Zacharias fell prostrate on the floor and didn't move, to the point that people wondered if he was dead.

The prophet Ezekiel said that in the presence of the Lord and at the vision the Lord gave him, he collapsed on the floor. The voice that called to him had to tell him to get up, saying, "Son of man, stand upon thy feet, and I will speak unto thee" (Ezekiel 2:1).

On the isle of Patmos, John said that he looked and saw Jesus standing in the midst of seven golden candlesticks. His voice sounded like the voice of many waters and His feet looked as if they were burning with fire. John wrote, "And when I saw him, I fell at his feet as dead" (Revelation 1:17).

Those who exalt themselves are humbled by the Lord.

Those who humble themselves before the Lord are those whom the Lord raises up.

Paul begs the Ephesians to prostrate themselves before the Lord, to recognize that the more gifted they are, the more humble they must be. They must be continually aware and acknowledge fully that the power working in them is not their own human power or ability, but the power of the Holy One of God.

Most of us do not desire a position of lowliness. It goes against our human nature. And that's precisely God's point. Anything we achieve or accomplish in this life as a believer in Christ Jesus is *not* something we do on our own. It is the Holy Spirit who dwells in us and works through us to accomplish *His* purposes. The more we are humble before the Lord and recognize that the work is His work, the accomplishments are His accomplishments, and the rewards are His rewards, the more God can and does use us.

As lowly as Paul was in his spirit, he felt even more lowly because of a "thorn in the flesh" that the Lord allowed the enemy to place in his life. Paul clearly saw this thorn as something that kept him from exalting himself. After Paul had prayed three times for the Lord to remove this thorn from his life, he heard the Lord say to him:

> **M**y grace is sufficient for thee: for my strength is made perfect in weakness.
>
> 2 CORINTHIANS 12:9

Paul responded to this word from the Lord by saying:

> **M**ost gladly therefore will I rather glory in my infirmities, that the power of Christ may rest upon me.
> Therefore I take pleasure in infirmities, in reproaches, in necessities, in persecutions, in distresses for Christ's sake: for when I am weak, then am I strong.
>
> 2 CORINTHIANS 12:9-10

None of us know exactly what that thorn was in Paul's life. What we each know, however, is that life has thorns. They come in many shapes and forms. The thorn may be a problem child, a restless marriage, an affliction in the body. God seems to tailor-make thorns for various personalities. And while it is our privilege to pray for the removal of thorns — and in many cases God responds by removing them — we must also recognize that at times God has a purpose for the thorns. That purpose is to keep us lowly and meek so that He can manifest Himself through us.

The thorn is just painful enough and disturbing enough that we are reminded always that *God* is working in us and through us. We are not succeeding or achieving anything on our own power. That thorn deflates all the air that other people will try to pump into our heads. That thorn allows us to receive a compliment and yet not become exalted by it. In this way, we remain meek and humble and pliable in the hands of God.

## THE ULTIMATE GOAL

Paul presents to the Ephesians the goal of our walk in Christ Jesus: As we walk in the unity of the faith and the knowledge of the Son of God, we will mature "unto a perfect man, unto the measure of the stature of the fulness of Christ" (Ephesians 4:13). Certainly, this is a precise definition of what it means to walk responsibly in Christ Jesus.

But what is a perfect man? The world certainly has its definition of the perfect man or the perfect woman. God's definition, however, is that the perfect person acts just as Jesus Christ would act in any given situation or circumstance. The word "perfect" means mature, developed, and brought to the full manifestation of divine purpose expressed through humanity.

God is never content with the status quo of our lives. He is always making us, calling us, developing us, and growing us up into a greater and greater likeness of Christ Jesus. We aren't just walking through life for the sake of walking. We aren't on an aimless stroll. We are going somewhere!

We are being called to be like Jesus.

We are being developed so that our ministry to others will be like that of Jesus.

We are being given experiences and put into situations so that we might mature to the point where we have the same attitude, perspective, and discernment as Jesus.

Every day, in countless ways, God is designing methods and ways of bringing us to full maturity in Christ. God is building us up so that we are a more accurate reflection of His Son. When we know this, pursuing the call of God takes on new meaning. We are stunned by the wisdom of God: As we follow

His call we become conformed to the image of His
Son, and our walk becomes holy and pleasing in
His sight.

Our walk in Christ Jesus is the only walk that
satisfies the human soul. It is the only walk that
fulfills our purpose for being on this earth and brings
us ever closer to our Lord. Our walk in Christ is the
reason we were created. When we accept this truth
and live it, we bring glory to God by walking
responsibly in Christ Jesus.

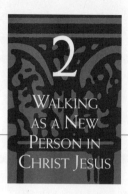

# 2

## WALKING AS A NEW PERSON IN CHRIST JESUS

As believers in Christ Jesus, we have the privilege of displaying the nature and characteristics of Jesus to people who do not yet know Him. It is an honor, but it is also a serious responsibility. In many instances, all people will know about Jesus is what they see as they observe our lives. Just telling people *about* Him is not enough. We are called to be witnesses *of* Him. It is how we act and react to situations which gives our neighbors and co-workers a negative or positive impression of Jesus.

I am always fascinated by how much unbelievers know about how Christians should live and act. If you don't believe this, just listen to what they say when believers behave badly, exhibit ungodly character, or act immorally. These worldly observers will say things like "I thought you were saved" or "I thought born-again people didn't...."

Our blessed position in Christ is a distinctive one. Believers cannot do, act, or say things like everyone else. We represent the Lord and His message of salvation. Understanding and accepting this reality can be difficult for some believers who do not like to be different.

## WE ARE DIFFERENT

Being different causes you to be noticed and exposed to scrutiny. Many people feel safe when they can hide in the crowd and be one of the gang, but hiding in the crowd is exactly what Jesus doesn't want us to do. In Matthew 5:16, He commanded us to let our light shine, and a shining light draws the attention of everything and everybody.

Believers walk in downtown areas and on Main Street, wearing the bright clothing of righteous living. However, for many, hidden underneath their clothes are struggles with desires and passions held over from their worldly life. Too often it is assumed that all is well with them because they look wholesome.

Some believers become comfortable living the double standard, enjoying the reputation of righteousness while continuing to dabble in the sins of the world. Of course, the common observation is that "everybody is doing it," but the truth is that everyone is *not* doing it — whatever *it* is. It doesn't matter if everybody is having sex with everybody else, everybody is cheating on their taxes, everybody is gossiping about their neighbors, or everybody is lying about nearly everything. We are called to live by a higher standard. We are no longer part of "everybody." We are part of the body of Christ Jesus.

All of us want to be liked by others. All of us want to be understood, welcomed, appreciated, and embraced by others. But if we are in Christ, we are going to have to face the fact that people in the world aren't going to understand us and many aren't going to like us. We are going to have to become dis-yoked, dislodged, and even disloyal to some people.

This has nothing to do with unity within the body of Christ. With other believers we are to become like-minded and of one heart. But with unbelievers who are living apart from Christ Jesus and are walking in darkness, we cannot be unified with them in their lawless thinking, attitudes, and practices. Paul exhorts us:

> *This I say therefore, and testify in the Lord, that ye henceforth walk not as other Gentiles walk, in the vanity of their mind,*
>
> *Having the understanding darkened, being alienated from the life of God through the ignorance that is in them, because of the blindness of their heart:*

*Who being past feeling have given themselves over unto lasciviousness, to work all uncleanness with greediness.*

EPHESIANS 4:17-19

Paul gives us a thorough and insightful description of how unbelievers walk. He says they walk "in the vanity of their mind," which means their minds are devoid of truth. When it comes to the Gospel and the kingdom of God, they are incapable of making an appropriate decision. Because they have hardened their hearts to God and are alienated from Him, we can have no spiritual fellowship with them.

## WALKING IN THE LIGHT

Paul draws a strong comparison between ignorance and darkness and also between light and knowledge. To be ignorant in spiritual matters is to live in darkness, which results in nothing but groping, grasping, and aimlessness. The person who walks around in the dark is a person who doesn't know where he is going or what he is about to trip over. Such a person is likely to be filled with frustration, confusion, and fear.

There are countless people on the earth today who have the capacity to be brilliant. They could be building spaceships and curing diseases and establishing companies, but they are ignorant. They haven't been taught what must be known in order to build a spaceship, cure a disease, or establish a successful company. Because they don't know, they live in a condition that is far less than their capacity.

So it is with those who live in spiritual darkness. They don't know they can have purpose and direction in their lives. They don't know all the wonderful things God has planned and prepared for them. They don't know the purpose God has for them, or how to walk in that purpose.

The reason they don't know is because they have chosen *not* to know. It isn't a matter of nobody teaching or nobody preaching or nobody available for wise counsel. It is because they have decided they simply don't want to know. Furthermore, this state of not knowing is not benign. This malignant arrogance that says, "I don't need to know" is flaunted in the public arena. Their influence is so pervasive that even some believers are caught up in the web of deceit they spin.

How many people who control the airwaves and wield great influence over the media and technology are people who are actually blind when it comes to why they are alive? Those who are alienated from God are not some sort of neutral entity that can be avoided. Paul says we are *not* to walk as these spiritually blind people walk. We are to avoid their influence. We are to reject the dark messages they constantly launch against our minds.

Too many times we hear people say, "Well, everybody believes that," or "Everybody is saying it," and the conclusion that is drawn is this: "Everybody must be right." No — everybody might be absolutely *wrong* if everybody is walking in spiritual darkness!

## WALK WITH RESTRAINT

I am a great proponent of the idea that it's time some Christians moved behind enemy lines. We need more truly saved, Christian reporters. We need more Christian magazines, more Christians creating television programs, more Christians involved in the leadership of companies and working as our representatives at all levels of government. But they are not to walk as the Gentiles walk. After Paul describes the incredible darkness in which those who do not know Jesus walk in Ephesians 4:17-19, he exhorts us:

> **B**ut ye have not so learned Christ.
>
> EPHESIANS 4:20

It's time Christians spoke up when evil raises its ugly head and attempts to steal our minds and destroy our homes with sexual immorality and mindless violence. It's time we refuse to be intimidated by those who simply don't know anything about spiritual reality and truth. We are to walk among the Gentiles, but we are not to be like them.

Nobody wants to be led by a blind guide. Nobody wants to follow an ignorant person. And yet daily, millions of Christians choose to be led by the blind guides of this world, those who are spiritually ignorant and who choose not to open their hearts to the Gospel of Christ Jesus.

Paul wrote to the Ephesians that these blind Gentiles are "past feeling" and have "given themselves over unto lasciviousness, to work all uncleanness with greediness" (Ephesians 4:19). "Lasciviousness" is unbridled lust, excess, and shamelessness — which all lead to unrestrained appetite. It is saying that we can do whatever we feel like doing whenever we feel like doing it without consequence.

Multiple sexual partners. Bisexual and homosexual relationships. Lust out of control. Husbands hitting wives. Wives murdering husbands. Children suffering from all kinds of abuse. Anger out of control. Drugs sold at every intersection, not only in the projects but in the suburbs and in the school corridors. Everybody high on something or addicted to something. A desire to escape reality gone out of control. That's unrestrained appetite.

Paul also states that the Gentiles have given themselves "to work all uncleanness with greediness" (Ephesians 4:19). The darkened, spiritually blind mind is a mind that is obsessed and addicted to things that are unclean before God. Furthermore, they see great gain and profit in the business of sin. For example, they earn a living by making pornographic films, selling drugs, getting involved in prostitution, or engaging in any kind of illegal, immoral, or unholy activity just because the money is good. To do so is to "work all uncleanness with greediness."

I have heard Christians say, "Well, I'll make money selling liquor and then give my profits to the church." That's a blind Gentile way of thinking! The same is true for those who bring injury to other people solely for the sake of gaining great profit for themselves. An honest profit does not bring harm or perpetuate sin.

In Ephesians 4:20, Paul says plainly that we have not learned this from Jesus. Jesus did not walk this way, and we are to be like Him. We are to restrain ourselves from these evil ways as He did, by the power of God's Word and the Holy Spirit within us. As believers, we have been taught and are continually being taught by the Holy Spirit. Jesus called the Holy Spirit the "Spirit of truth," and He said that the Spirit would lead us into every remembrance of His Word that we needed to make wise decisions.

Some may say, "Well, I don't know that much about the Bible. I'm a new believer. I haven't known Jesus very long." No matter how long you have known Jesus Christ, there are some things you are going to *know* immediately as being right or wrong through the leading of the Holy Spirit. There is an immediate awareness once a person has received Jesus Christ as Savior that certain behaviors and certain attitudes are no longer appropriate to our new way of life. Then, as we continue to study God's Word, we will discover that the leading of the Holy Spirit is always in complete concert with His Word, that the Word of God is not a dead letter filled with impossible demands, but alive and full of life-transforming power.

The Holy Spirit makes alive in us an understanding of what is corrupt, deceitful, lustful, and sinful. And as we renew our mind with the Word of God, our senses become more keen to discerning and differentiating between good and evil.

> **F**or every one that useth milk is unskilful in the word of righteousness: for he is a babe.
>
> But strong meat belongeth to them that are of full age, even those who by reason of use have their senses exercised to discern both good and evil.
>
> HEBREWS 5:13-14

**37**

In certain areas of vulnerability and weakness, we can insulate ourselves from failure only by submitting ourselves to the ministry and teaching we need to be set free and stay free. There's no excuse for any believer to remain blind to God's truth or to live like an unbeliever. If God has called us to restrain our flesh, then He has provided the means by which we can do it.

## PUT OFF THE OLD NATURE

A believer should never say, "I am now a part of the redeemed and forgiven, but I am living just the same way I lived before I accepted Jesus Christ as my Savior." Our lives are to be different than that of blind sinners. There are some things that we *put off* when we come to Christ.

> *If so be that ye have heard him, and have been taught by him, as the truth is in Jesus:*
>
> *That ye put off concerning the former conversation the old man, which is corrupt according to the deceitful lusts.*
>
> EPHESIANS 4:21-22

The phrase "put off" is a vivid picture of a person taking off their filthy rags of sin and self-righteousness and burning them. They do not take them off and hang them in the closet for a rainy, difficult day; nor do they just toss them on the floor to be tripped over daily. That is a perfect illustration of deceitful lusts. For example, we cannot go drinking with our associates from work, all the while claiming we are being a light. The truth is, we are walking in darkness.

No, when we take off our filthy rags, we are to rid ourselves forever of all thinking, attitudes, and behavior associated with our existence apart from Jesus Christ. This is an outward manifestation of the inward transformation, what the Bible calls the fruit of righteousness. (See Hebrews 12:11 and James 3:18.) Earlier we discussed believers who walk on Main Street with clothes of righteousness but underneath are filled with turmoil. The process whereby they rid themselves of this contradiction is the putting off and burning forever the undergarments of sin.

God does not automatically remove every evil thing from our lives the moment we receive Jesus as Lord and Savior. We still have baggage and bondage left over from our former life which we must remove and destroy. It is our responsibility to put off those things. We may not want to acknowledge that we have them in us, clinging to us, or flowing from us. We may not even want to talk about them. But eventually we are going to have to face them, because *we cannot put on the new man and be the new person we are in Christ if we are holding on to the old man.*

There are many believers who have old habits they need to break. Some of those habits are prejudices and old ways of thinking. Some of those habits are so common to a person's life that they aren't even aware they have them. But one by one, those habits must be changed. Some believers have broken their old habits, but they still are tormented by the thoughts related to them. They are tormented in their minds. These thoughts have to be put off just as much as the habits.

> **F**inally, brethren, whatsoever things are true, whatsoever things are honest, whatsoever things are just, whatsoever things are pure, whatsoever things are lovely, whatsoever things are of good report; if there be any virtue, and if there be any praise, think on these things.
>
> Those things, which you have both learned, and received, and heard, and seen in me, do: and the God of peace shall be with you.
>
> PHILIPPIANS 4:8-9

We can only successfully and permanently put off thoughts by replacing them with godly thoughts. We must reassure ourselves of God's unfailing commitment to our future by becoming extremely familiar with His promises in His Word. We must train our minds to think about things other than the sin in which we once lived. We need to start building new habits of thinking which will then help us to establish godly attitudes, behavior, and reactions.

**A**nd be renewed in the spirit of your mind;
And that ye put on the new man, which after God
is created in righteousness and true holiness.

EPHESIANS 4:23-24

There are some rich nuggets of thought in the phrase "renewed in the spirit of your mind." The word "mind" is not the word for brain, but rather refers to the manner in which a person comes to conclusions. It is the ability to perceive, understand, and to feel, judge, and determine things. Paul says that we are to make new or young again the attitude of our thinking. How we process information and the manner in which we come to conclusions must be subject to the will of God.

When a person starts thinking new thoughts or putting on new habits, they may feel a little strange at first. They may think, "This is just a put on!" Just as a new coat or a new pair of shoes may not be immediately comfortable, so our new thoughts and new habits may not immediately feel natural to us. What we must do, however, is to continue putting on those new thoughts and new habits that we know are right before God again and again until they are comfortable!

We have to practice being nice until we are automatically nice.

We have to practice going to church every Sunday morning until anything but church on Sunday morning seems strange to us.

We have to practice giving our financial gifts in the offering until giving to God is as natural as buying a new outfit at the mall.

We have to practice speaking the truth until a lie tastes bad in our mouths and telling the truth is our automatic response when we are questioned in any situation.

We must practice giving people good words until our old cynical, sarcastic, negative, bitter, and angry remarks are completely purged from our conversations.

"But," you may say, "isn't this hypocritical — feeling one way and speaking and doing something else?"

No. It's *retraining* yourself to walk the way the Lord desires for you to walk and *restraining* yourself from lasciviousness. You are declaring to Him, "It's no longer a matter of anything goes in my life. It's a matter of what You say and what You command and what You direct me to do."

## FOUR THINGS WE MUST PUT OFF

In Ephesians 4:21-24, Paul tells us flat out that any change in our behavior requires our will. What we do is our choice. Paul is very specific with the

Ephesians — and us — about what must be put off
and what must be put on:

> **W**herefore putting away lying, speak every man truth
> with his neighbor: for we are members one of another.
>
> Be ye angry, and sin not: let not the sun go down
> upon your wrath:
>
> Neither give place to the devil.
>
> Let him that stole steal no more: but rather let him
> labour, working with his hands the thing which is
> good, that he may have to give to him that needeth.
>
> Let no corrupt communication proceed out of your
> mouth, but that which is good to the use of edifying,
> that it may minister grace unto the hearers.
>
> EPHESIANS 4:25-29

**No More Lying.** Lying has to go. In its place we
must put on truth. Lying is conscious and inten-
tional falsehood, a deliberate attempt to deceive, to
convince a person of something that is not true or
of a feeling that is not genuine.

Lying is anything that is not the "whole truth and
nothing but the truth" in both content and intent. It
includes those little lies that some people are so quick
to justify. Lying includes leading others to a false
conclusion, even though we may not actually have
spoken false words. It includes setting up a pretense
or an illusion that is false. In the place of lying we
must become truth seekers and truth speakers.

**No More Sinning in Anger.** Unrestrained anger that results in sinful behavior has to go. In its place, we are to reach for reconciliation and peace.

Paul is not talking about righteous indignation or being angry at sin and taking a stand for what is right. Nor is he talking about ignoring evil and refusing to do anything about it. God has given us the ability to feel anger so that we will get angry at the same things that anger Him — the misuse and abuse and "use" of people for evil.

We are to be angry whenever and wherever we find sin in operation and the devil in charge. But we are to respond to those situations that make us angry by engaging in the spiritual warfare necessary for bringing down the strongholds of Satan. We are not to seek revenge for ourselves or those who have been hurt or offended. Paul is very clear that anger isn't a sin in and of itself. What is wrong is being angry and then sinning in our anger.

We are to go immediately to those with whom we have quarrels and disagreements and to reconcile our differences — even before nightfall. We are to give the devil absolutely no place to hang his hat in our lives. We are to give him no toehold, no crack in the door of our soul. We are to completely turn a deaf ear to any temptation the devil whispers to entice us to sin in anger.

**No More Stealing.** "Let him that stole steal no more" (Ephesians 4:28). In the place of stealing, Paul says, "Go get a job. Do something good. Earn so that you have something to give away."

Paul knew that Ephesus was a major trade city of the world. It was a city where everybody was out for a deal and out to gain as much profit as possible. It was a city with great wealth, a lot of buying and selling, a lot of caravans and ships bringing their wares. It also had a lot of corruption and greed.

There's a big connection between stealing and hoarding. Those who steal from others, which includes those who cheat, are dishonest, and underhanded, are "me" centered people. They want everything flowing their way. Once they have obtained something from others through immoral and illegal means, they are very unlikely to let loose of it. They consume what they steal or they spend what they steal on themselves. Why? Because they are continually trying to prove to themselves that they deserve what they have stolen. They are continually trying to possess it in order to lay rightful claim to it. The more they steal, the tighter they hold on to what they steal in order to make sure they are in possession of it. The truth is, of course, that they can never lay full claim because what they are seeking to claim is not rightfully theirs.

Another reason people who steal are stingy is because they have stolen in their own power. God never helps a person steal! God is totally against stealing, and again, that includes dishonesty, greed, and cheating. Those who steal are never quite sure when another opportunity will come along to steal, and therefore, they cling tightly to what they have, keeping it totally for themselves.

There's a similar link between earning and giving. Those who earn things through honest means know that what they have is rightfully theirs to do with as they desire. They are much more likely to give extra to those in need whenever they can.

They also know that whatever they have earned is by the grace of God. God helps those who are engaged in honest labor. He rewards those who labor "as unto Him." Those who work honestly are in a position to obey the command of Jesus, "Freely ye have received, freely give" (Matthew 10:8). They know they can trust God to continue to help them earn and work and give. God is in that cycle and, therefore, the cycle will continue.

Paul is not only trying to clean up thievery and dishonesty, he's trying to turn around the entire way the Ephesians think and behave toward one another. He's preaching a spirit of generosity to the Church — a free-flowing sharing of gifts.

Why is this spirit of generosity so important in the Church? Because it relates to far more than practical gifts of money and material possessions. It includes the gifts of the Spirit. It includes ministry to others. It includes sharing the Gospel. It includes witnessing about Jesus Christ. If you are truly a generous person, you are going to be a person who is willing to turn yourself inside out for other people. You'll turn your pockets inside out to give. You'll turn your schedule upside down so you have time to give. You'll open the doors of your home so you can give hospitality. You'll open up every treasure chest of talent or skill you have been given to enrich the lives of others.

A truly generous person is a person the Holy Spirit can use. A generous person is an open vessel, an open conduit through which He can move. The generous person is a person through whom the Holy Spirit can pour His gifts and manifest His fruit.

Are you committed to earning as much as you can — in right ways, with a right spirit and motivation, in a right job — so that you can give as much as you can to others in the name of Jesus? We need to be committed to earning in that way. Imagine what a blessing could be poured out to our churches, our neighborhoods, our cities, and to needy areas around the world if all believers were this generous!

**No More Corrupt Communication.** Paul says, "Stop talking like you used to talk. Stop engaging in anything that causes decay, destruction, or 'dirt' to be generated in another person's life. Instead, speak good words to and about others."

Corrupt communication is not simply swearing and telling dirty jokes — neither of which have a part in the walk of a believer. Corrupt communication means communication that has become twisted, polluted, and invalid. Corrupt communication is lying. It is any form of communication that leads to an end that is contrary to God's highest and best desires for another person.

Are you aware that cynicism, sarcasm, and negative criticism are all forms of corrupt communication? These types of communication tell only your opinion about a matter, which is never the genuine truth of the matter from God's point of view. Cynical, sarcastic, critical comments tear a person down just as much as a blatant lie about that person can tear down their reputation or their self-esteem. They can cause a part of that person's esteem to be struck down or part of their spiritual growth in Christ Jesus to become paralyzed.

Paul tells the Ephesians to speak only "that which is good to the use of edifying, that it may minister grace unto the hearers" (Ephesians 4:29). Edifying means "to build up." It doesn't mean false flattery or praise, but to build up another person in the spirit. It means to speak God's Word to them without any overtones of self-righteousness or condemnation. It means to give genuine compliments because we recognize that they are the workmanship of God and someone to whom God has poured out His grace, love, and mercy.

To edify is to recognize that another person has just as much claim to the grace of God as we have. The attitude behind edification is that another person is in just as much need of forgiveness and has just as much access to forgiveness as we have. To edify is to say things that will help a person hold their head up just a little higher, walk just a little straighter, and act just a little bit better than before.

We should never justify hurtful conversation just because it is the truth. Never does the Bible tell you to tell everything you know! In fact, many of the proverbs are adamant that only a fool tells their whole mind all the time. If the telling of a fact is going to tear up the unity of the body or bring down another person, it's wrong to voice that fact. Let that fact die within you and allow God to do what He desires to do without your adding the fuel of your words to a verbal bonfire.

There's no room in a believer's walk to say, "Well, I got my mama's tongue and I've just got to say what I think." The fact is, your mama's tongue might have been corrupt. What you are thinking may not be true. James said this, "Whoever controls the tongue, controls the whole movement of the body." (See James 3:3-5.) To a great extent, what you say determines the extent of your ability to act. It puts a boundary on what you can do and will do, and it sets limits on your witness.

We think, we speak, we act. That is the usual progression of human behavior. But it is not only ourselves that we influence when we speak. We are also putting limits on others, and ultimately upon the body of Christ as a whole. What we say exerts influence upon the entire body of believers with whom we are in association!

A little statement of gossip not only corrupts the speaker of that gossip, but it brings damage to the ears of the persons who hear it and to the reputation of the person about whom the gossip is being spread. It causes a chain reaction to go into effect in three directions — speaker, hearer, and victim — that spreads evil tentacles of destruction through the community or the church in which those people live.

A little lie not only brings damage to the soul of the liar, but it causes the hearer of that lie to be damaged and infected with falsehood. The person who hears a lie may act on that lie, believing it to be true. Those actions will also be false. They, in turn, will impact other people, and bit by bit the entire community or church has been infected with an element of falsehood and decay. What we say has ripple effects — powerful ripple effects that reach far beyond us to affect the lives of others.

In contrast, to give an edifying word is to say something that will help a person see Jesus more clearly, desire a deeper relationship with the Father, and be more open to the Holy Spirit. To give an edifying word causes a person to open themselves to *all* that God desires to do in their lives and through their lives.

Edifying words also have ripple effects — powerful ones that can bring about good. Edifying words flowing through a body of believers bring about a greater outpouring of love, acceptance, forgiveness, and reconciliation. Edifying words spoken frequently in a group of believers produce unity and, in unity, greater spiritual power. Edifying words create an atmosphere where lives are changed and blessings are poured out.

## WE CAN DO IT!

Paul would not have begged the Ephesians to give up lying, stealing, anger, and corrupt communication if this manner of life was impossible for us to achieve. The fact is, we *can* live this way. We don't have to tell lies in order to advance our position, steal from others to be prosperous, or be dishonest in order to gain what we need. We do not have to be angry in order to exert control or engage in corrupt communication to get our way. Simply put, we do not have to give place to the devil!

We can walk in "righteousness and true holiness" (Ephesians 4:24). It's a choice we make daily as we pray, "Holy Spirit, lead me. Holy Spirit, help me to guard my tongue. Help me to earn and to give. Guide me into the right ways in which to express my anger at injustice and evil. Help me to become a mighty warrior in assaulting the gates of hell."

When we choose to live this way, according to God's Word and by the power and leading of the Holy Spirit, an exciting and world-changing reality occurs. We are literally *being* the new person we are in Christ Jesus. We are living from our true essence and eternal identity, and our walk with Jesus becomes a daily adventure in faith and power!

# 3

## WALKING IN STRENGTH

The book of Ephesians was written from a prison cell in Rome several years after Paul's last meeting with the church leadership from Ephesus. Paul had lived and worked in Ephesus for three years, and for two of those years he had taught daily in the school of a believer named Tyrannus. (See Acts 19:8-10.) He was no stranger to the Ephesians and they were no strangers to him. He knew them and the issues that faced them.

Paul had enjoyed a powerful ministry among the Ephesians and many miracles took place. This is where handkerchiefs and aprons were taken from his body and the sick were delivered from diseases and evil spirits when those handkerchiefs and aprons were laid on them. (See Acts 19:11-12.) It was in Ephesus that so many were converted to Jesus Christ that a vast number of pagan scrolls and instruments of magic were burned. (See Acts 19:17-19.) There were so many that received Jesus that the silversmiths who made shrines to the goddess Diana brought the whole city to a riot because they were so upset at their loss of sales. (See Acts 19:23-41.) Nevertheless, despite the persecution and rioting, the Gospel flourished. In Acts 19:20 we read, "So mightily grew the word of God and prevailed."

## PAUL'S FAREWELL: DEFENSIVE STRATEGY

In Acts 20:16, Paul was on his way to Jerusalem to celebrate Pentecost when he stopped at the port of Miletus to meet with the elders of the church at Ephesus. During this last and brief time with them, Paul reminded them of many things, but when we examine this passage of Scripture in detail, we see clearly how Paul leaves the Ephesians with a word from God on how to defend themselves and stand strong in the faith at all times, "at all seasons." He reminds them that for the years he lived among them, he overcame every temptation and trial he faced and how he accomplished this superhuman feat.

*And from Miletus he sent to Ephesus, and called the elders of the church.*

*And when they were come to him, he said unto them, Ye know, from the first day that I came into Asia, after what manner I have been with you at all seasons,*

*Serving the Lord with all humility of mind, and with many tears, and temptations, which befell me by the lying in wait of the Jews:*

*And how I kept back nothing that was profitable unto you, but have shewed you, and have taught you publicly, and from house to house,*

*Testifying both to the Jews and also to the Greeks, repentance toward God, and faith toward our Lord Jesus Christ.*

ACTS 20:17-21

First, the *manner* in which Paul served the Lord and the Ephesians was "with all humility of mind." This is the attitude of lowliness and meekness Paul exhorts us to have in Ephesians 4:2, which we discussed in chapter 1. When we maintain an attitude of humility, the Holy Spirit can teach us and strengthen us. We will have the wisdom and God's supernatural power to prevail over the temptations and trials that come against us. But if we are proud and arrogant, the Holy Spirit can do nothing with us and we are left to our own thinking and ability. It is inevitable that we will fail and fall.

Second, Paul "kept back nothing that was profitable unto you, but have showed you, and have taught you publicly, and from house to house." Not only did he teach them everything they needed to know to succeed as Christians in a very hostile, dangerous world, but he lived it in front of them twenty-four hours a day. Paul didn't preach one thing on Sunday and then live contrary to his message on Monday. He went from house to house and *showed* them what it meant to live victoriously and holy for Jesus Christ.

More than that, when Paul messed up, when his carnal thinking or fleshly desires overtook him or the devil's craftiness succeeded in distracting or deceiving him for a time, he was quick to repent, "Testifying both to the Jews, and also to the Greeks, repentance toward God, and faith toward our Lord Jesus Christ." This third point cannot be overemphasized!

When men and women of God who are leaders in the body of Christ are overtaken by a fault before those they lead, when fathers and mothers miss the mark in their families, and when employers sin against God and against their employees, it is absolutely imperative that they come to repentance before those who follow them. Why is this so vital? When a standard of purity and excellence is lifted up by leaders, parents, and employers, it can then be passed down through the ranks of leadership in the body of Christ so that every member maintains purity and excellence. Then the whole body can be "fitly joined together" and every "joint can supply." (See Ephesians 4:16.)

Your physical body is not going to be able to do  much if your shoulder or your knee or your elbow is out of joint, and the body of Christ is no different in a spiritual sense. If we are going to succeed in the calling God has given us, if we are going to reach the lost, heal the sick, cast the devil out, and make disciples, we must be healthy and all our joints must be supplying.

> **A**nd now, behold, I know that ye all, among whom I have gone preaching the kingdom of God, shall see my face no more.
> Wherefore I take you to record this day, that I am pure from the blood of all men.
> For I have not shunned to declare unto you all the counsel of God.

> ACTS 20:25-27

Paul now makes a monumental statement: He is pure from the blood of all men because he has not neglected his most sacred duty and holy responsibility before God, which is to declare the whole counsel of God. In other words, Paul was careful to feed the flock of God with a balanced diet of the Word.

There is a tendency in the contemporary church for pastors and leaders to specialize in one area of the Gospel or the kingdom. While it is exciting to see God operate in certain areas like healing, prosperity, or worship, a congregation must also be nourished by the principles of righteousness, spiritual warfare, and holiness. It is balanced and comprehensive teaching in the Word of God that equips believers with the strength and overall stability to successfully withstand the assaults of the devil as they walk with God. Satan is cunning and does not attack in one way at all times. He uses different strategies and weapons to penetrate our greatest weakness at just the right moment.

Our revelation and practice of worship from yesterday may not overcome and defeat the forces of darkness that will come against us tomorrow. Healing scriptures alone may not keep our house built on the rock when the storms of deception rage against us. We must continually grow in the Word as the Spirit of God leads us to study the whole counsel of God. And pastors and leaders must be diligent to teach the whole counsel of God as the Spirit leads. Only the Holy Spirit knows what we need to learn today that will sustain us tomorrow.

Paul then went on to give a strong warning:

> **T**ake heed therefore unto yourselves, and to all the flock, over the which the Holy Ghost hath made you overseers, to feed the church of God, which he hath purchased with his own blood.
>
> For I know this, that after my departing shall grievous wolves enter in among you, not sparing the flock.
>
> ACTS 20:28-29

Paul knew that the Church would always be opposed by somebody, over something, at some time. No local church founded on the shed blood of Jesus Christ has ever been established without facing opposition. No body of believers has ever become so mature in the faith that all opposition has disappeared. The wolves are out there...ravenous and vicious. Paul's desire is that the believers in Ephesus and today be *wolf-proofed*.

What counts is not the fact that we live without adversity, but rather, that we have the strength to stand strong in the face of it. That is the real crux of the matter. Paul is determined that his ministry will outlive him, and in order for that to happen, the church at Ephesus must remain strong when opposing voices rise up.

Our concern today is that we be so rooted and grounded and established in the truth that *we* will stand when opposition comes our way. If we rely upon the crutches of fantasy and a false sense of well-being, when the adversary attacks, we will be quick to crumble because our crutches are flimsy. Crutches are hollow and paper thin. Only the truth of God's Word will hold us steady and steadfast when the storms come.

It is never realistic to think that a person can do anything for God — including living a steadfast

Christian life in the midst of daily challenges — and not face intense opposition on a regular basis. The Church must build a strong line of defense with God's Word to stand strong against the wolves from within and without. Paul said to the Ephesians:

> **A**lso of your own selves shall men arise, speaking perverse things, to draw away disciples after them.
> Therefore watch, and remember, that by the space of three years I ceased not to warn every one night and day with tears.

ACTS 20:30-31

Opposition is not only from the outside, but also from inside the Church. A split in a church is nothing new. From the very beginning, Paul antici-pated divisions, "isms," and schisms. He said to the Ephesian elders, "I've got to prepare you for those things before they arise, so you will be strong. Please remember how I tearfully and continuously warned you of these things for the three years I was with you."

Paul labored among the Ephesians for their benefit, even to the point of weeping before God both for them and with them that they might grow strong in the Lord Jesus Christ. He was determined that they have sufficient enduring strength to sustain their faith after he was gone. Paul was not a man who spewed religious rhetoric from cold lips

and an indifferent heart. He had passion for his
students. He made himself available to them day
and night.

> **A**nd now, brethren, I commend you to God, and to
> the word of his grace, which is able to build you up, and
> to give you an inheritance among all them which are
> sanctified (those who are set apart for His use).

ACTS 20:32, addition mine

Paul had absolute confidence that the Word of
God was able to equip the Church with all it
needed to withstand any assault. He had so much
confidence in the strengthening power of God's
Word that he was able to leave the elders of
Ephesus on the dock at Miletus with full assurance
and every confidence that they would be all right.
He knew he would never see them again on this
earth, but that the Word of God would continue to
build them up in his absence.

Paul closed his comments to these elders of the
early church by saying, "I have shewed you all
things, how that so labouring ye ought to support
the weak" (Acts 20:35). He wanted them to follow
his example — to teach, to build up, to support, to
give all that they had to the challenge of remaining
strong in Christ. And after he had spoken his heart
fully to them, he prayed with them and said good-
bye in a very emotional parting.

*And when he had thus spoken, he kneeled down, and prayed with them all.*

*And they all wept sore, and fell on Paul's neck, and kissed him,*

*Sorrowing most of all for the words which he spake, that they should see his face no more. And they accompanied him unto the ship.*

ACTS 20:36-38

These people loved Paul and Paul loved them. It was out of his great love for them that he pleaded with them, "Continue in God's Word always. The Word is your only line of defense in this world. It will keep you strong and allow you to prevail over every evil thing, including the wolves who come to your door or perverse deceivers who rise up among you. Don't waver from the truth!"

## RETAKING OCCUPIED TERRITORY

Walking in strength is not only a defensive measure, but it is also an offensive tactic. We explored how to use the strength of God to protect ourselves from the ravages of wolves; now we are prepared to march forward and offensively and aggressively take back what the enemy has stolen.

When it comes to walking in strength, Ephesians and Joshua are companion books. The book of Joshua presents a story of conquest. Armed with

the anointing of God and His mandate to take the
Promised Land, Joshua and the Israelites exercised
their freedom and calling to be kingdom builders
for the first time. In the same way, Paul beseeches
the Ephesians to do more than just "hold the fort."
He said to them,

> I commend you to God, and to the word of his
> grace, which is able to build you up, and to give you
> an inheritance among all them which are sanctified
> (those who are set apart for His use).
>
> ACTS 20:32, addition mine

We are set apart for His use and we have an
inheritance to obtain! We do not merely sit
and count our blessings and expect everything
we need and want to just fall out of heaven.
We are to rise up on our most holy faith and
march forward to take back what the devil has
stolen and to take hold of that which God has
already purchased for us through the blood of
Jesus Christ. Like the Israelites in Joshua, we
must garner all our strength and courage from
the knowledge that God is on our side and
what He says we have, we can have.

After Paul builds us up in the first chapters of
Ephesians, expounding on the truths of our calling,
election, and intimacy with God, he then stirs the
nest like a mother eagle, prompting us to take
wings and fly. Otherwise, we will never realize the

majestic heights to which we have been called, the destiny that awaits us.

Believers were never intended by God to be the recipients of salvation alone. While it is true that we have been saved from death, we have also been saved to life — abundant life. Being saved from death is a simple case of rescue, but God is interested in more than just rescuing us. He has chosen to make us partners and joint heirs of all that He intended for us to share with Him from the beginning, that we might move out in His power and reclaim the bounty of those riches which lay strewn on the fields of the promised land.

From our perspective as New Testament believers, the book of Joshua is a picture of people who have ceased from wandering in desert places, who have come to know God, who have embraced the promises of God, and who are now ready to seize the things that God has promised to them.

The book of Joshua is not a book for wimps, and neither is the book of Ephesians. Ephesians is not for wanderers — those who wander from this conviction to that, murmuring and complaining along the way, backsliding as much as they are moving forward, always with one eye looking back to Egypt. If you still have a desire for life in Egypt, a life of sin and compromise, then you are not ready to march in and seize the promised land!

Let me be very practical here. I have met people who tell me that they have no problem watching certain television programs that are filled with lustful and violent messages. As far as I am concerned, these people are giving the devil the sofa in their living room. They are allowing him to occupy that place. They may have shut the devil out of every other place in their lives, but they allow him to reside and rule there.

I have met other people who say, "Well, business is business and business is cutthroat. It's highly competitive. Certain tactics are required to succeed." These people are giving the devil a place in their office. They are allowing the devil to sit across the desk from them and to conduct his business there, his way. They may have claimed every other area of their lives as a place for righteousness, but not their office place.

I have met other people who say, "Church is church, but then there's my sex life." These people put on holy clothes on Sunday morning and are just as quick to take them off on Sunday night with someone who is not their spouse. They don't see any relationship between their sexuality and their spirituality. They have allowed the devil to claim this territory in their lives.

It is God's desire that we take back ALL that the devil has occupied!

When Joshua prepared to enter the land of Canaan, he had a full awareness that every square inch of that land was held by the enemy. Not one city, not one acre had been claimed by the Israelites. God had promised it to them, but it still was not theirs. It could only be theirs if they would take it.

Just as Joshua and the Israelites had to drive back the Hittites and Jebusites and other people who represented the worst sins of mankind, so you are going to have to drive the devil out of every square inch of the territory of your life. While you were living in a state of sin, the devil took over vast areas — in some people, he took over just about every area! Now that you are saved, whenever the devil has an opportunity, he is going to move in and take control in those areas. He is going to occupy your sexual desires, your desires for things, your desire for power, and your desire for wealth.

John wrote that we are to stop loving the world and "all that is in the world, the lust of the flesh, and the lust of the eyes, and the pride of life" (1 John 2:15-16). When we begin our walk as believers in

Christ Jesus, God gives us the strength to *remove* the devil from our lives and take back every inch of territory he has occupied.

Taking over the territory of the devil means...

...kicking the devil out of your house — every room of your house, every bookshelf of your house, every shelf of your cupboards, every nook and cranny, including the space under the bed!

...kicking the devil out of your car and refusing to let him ride with you.

...kicking the devil out of your neighborhood and out of your church.

...kicking the devil out of the place where you work so that you do your job as unto the Lord and in righteousness.

...kicking the devil out of your social life and refusing to associate with those who exert influence over you to commit sin or evil deeds.

...kicking the devil out of your marriage relationship so that you no longer pattern your marriage after the world, but after God's Word.

...kicking the devil out of your love life and putting an end to illicit affairs and ungodly romances.

...kicking the devil out of your family, so that the devil no longer has control or influence over your children.

...kicking the devil out of your viewing habits, your reading habits, your spending habits, and your consumption habits.

Now, the devil is not going to just roll over and give up without a fight! He is going to fight you over every bit of territory. He isn't going to give up easily. He desires to rule this world, both the territory of the world and the systems of the world. He doesn't care anything about the people of the world — ever! The fact is, the devil ends up destroying the people he influences and who are under his power. He steals from them, lies to them, and eventually kills them.

The good news is that once God has liberated us, we are given the power to drive the enemy out of our land! The Bible says that we have the authority to say to the devil, "You may not occupy this place anymore. You have no authority here. You have no right to be here. Get out in the name of Jesus!"

Once you are a believer in Christ Jesus, you are called to walk out the land that God has promised to you and to regain every aspect of your life in Christ. Just as Joshua and the Israelites were given the authority, the power, and the ability to take Jericho, you have been given the authority, the power, and the ability to cause certain walls to go tumbling down in your life. You have the ability to tear down the very strongholds of Satan and to  declare, "Devil, I no longer belong to you. I belong to Jesus Christ."

It's time we say to the devil...

"You can't have my rest and my peace, because God gives His beloved sleep." (See Psalm 127:2.)

"You can't have my healing and health, because by Jesus' stripes I was healed." (See 1 Peter 2:24.)

"You can't have my mind and my imagination, because I cast down every imagination and thought that exalts itself against the knowledge of God." (See 2 Corinthians 10:5.)

Nervous breakdown? Unacceptable! I can do all things through Jesus Christ! (See Philippians 4:13.)

Marriage breakdown? No way! Jesus is the author and finisher of my faith! (See Hebrews 12:2.)

Communication breakdown? Not necessary! God gives me wisdom! (See James 1:5.)

Our offensive weapon is the same as our defensive weapon — the sword of the Spirit, the Word of God. (See Ephesians 6:17.) Wherever and whenever you tell the devil he has to "get out of your way" and "get off your land" by speaking the Word of the Lord in the power of the Holy Spirit, he must go. You have the authority, the power, and the ability to successfully expel the enemy from your territory, which is any place your foot lands. God has called you to walk in His strength today!

## 4
### WALKING IN UNITY

*I therefore, the prisoner of the Lord, beseech you that ye walk worthy of the vocation wherewith ye are called, With all lowliness and meekness, with longsuffering, forbearing one another in love;*
*Endeavouring to keep the unity of the Spirit in the bond of peace.*

EPHESIANS 4:1-3

Immediately after admonishing the believer to dignify the divine vocation with an appropriate lifestyle, Paul continues without pause to set the attitude in which we are to walk and the manner by which we walk. We don't walk alone. Not only do we have the Holy Spirit in us, but we have both the privilege and the responsibility of walking with others. There is no place in the Scriptures where we are called to live in isolation as *individuals* or to think we are the only *group* of people worthy of Christ. We are to "keep the unity of the Spirit in the bond of peace."

Paul is consumed with the importance of relationships, which comprise unity, and that is why he goes right into this issue after begging us to walk worthy of our calling. The truth is, fulfilling our calling is inseparably tied to our allegiance to one another. In chapter 4, he calls the Ephesians to be longsuffering toward one another, forbearing one another in love. This is the attitude we are to have as we walk. And for what purpose? "To keep the unity of the Spirit in the bond of peace." He is continually trying to bring about a oneness in the Church by encouraging believers to care for one another, be patient with one another, yield to one another, and bear the burdens of one another.

Let's consider this word "longsuffering." In the Greek text it is the word *makrothumia*. This is one of two words used primarily for patience and longsuffering. The other one is *hupomene*. *Hupomene* means "under alone" and suggests that we must be willing to stand under the pressure of the situation by ourselves. But *makrothumia* expresses the attitude of an endurance test. The word means "far away passion," suggesting that the person having *makrothumia* remains calm while going through a test, storm, or struggle because their passion is directed toward something beyond, something which transcends and outweighs any present discomfort.

We must have a passion for unity in the Church, because unity in the Church has a cost attached to it. It doesn't happen automatically or without effort. So often we think that if we just come together and love God, we are going to get along. But getting along takes effort. It takes a willingness to be long-suffering with one another, to diffuse our selfish ambitions and considerations and cast them over on God so that unity and peace can be sustained.

A passion for unity requires a conscious decision to stick together and not leave a group when things get difficult or if we encounter somebody we don't like. This is true also for a family or a marriage. If people are to live together in peace, they are going to have to achieve unity — and then make a constant effort to keep and guard the unity they have achieved.

## THE HOLY SPIRIT'S ROLE

*Unity apart from the Holy Spirit is impossible.*

In ourselves, we don't have enough love to be united in spirit with another person. We don't have the patience, the goodness, the kindness, the joy, or the self-control that is required. Those are aspects of the fruit of the Holy Spirit! It is only as we willfully and consciously decide that we are going to live and walk according to the Spirit that we can begin to achieve unity with other believers.

Why is it so important that we work for unity in the body of Christ? Because it is only in a unified body that the power of God can be released. It is only when we see ourselves tied together under the authority of the divine Chief Executive Officer that we begin to experience the fullness of the Holy Spirit's power flowing freely in our midst. It is the power of God that destroys the yoke of bondage — of sin, sickness, and oppression — and if there's one thing we need in the Church today, it is more of God's saving, delivering, and healing power!

> **B**ehold, how good and how pleasant it is for brethren to dwell together in unity!
>
> It is like the precious ointment upon the head, that ran down upon the beard, even Aaron's beard: that went down to the skirts of his garments.
>
> PSALM 133:1-2

This is a perfect picture of unity in the body of Christ. In your mind's eye you can see the oil as it is poured over the head, streams down the face and beard, makes its way to the hem of the garment and drips upon the feet until they glisten. This is the oil of gladness for the corporate body of believers. There is a joy and peace that come when believers are synchronized by the unifying power of God's anointing. Earlier we discussed walking in synchronized fashion with the Holy Spirit. Now we take this one step further and see that as we walk in this manner with the Spirit, we can walk in unity with one another.

When the leader of a particular church in the body of Christ is anointed with the Holy Spirit, that oil is to run from head to toe in that church without becoming the least bit diluted or polluted by individual agendas or fleshly desires in the church body. Thus, a sample of oil taken from the bottom of the skirt should be identical to a sample of oil taken from the top of the anointed one's head — pure and undefiled.

Any time you begin to inject your feelings, your opinions, your agenda, your goals, or your desires into the pure agenda of the Holy Spirit, you dilute and pollute what the Holy Spirit is attempting to do in you and in others with whom your life is linked. When that happens, unity corrodes and ministry becomes less and less effective. The presence and power of the Holy Spirit dissipates because He is grieved and is leaving.

How do we go about achieving and maintaining the Holy Spirit as the central life force in the body of Christ? It happens only when each believer is willing to submit themselves to the Holy Spirit and say, "What the Spirit is doing and what the Spirit is saying is far more important than my personal image, reputation, influence, or identity." We must see the unity of the Spirit as being essential to the power of God being released in us so that we can heal the brokenhearted and set the captives free. We must be willing to fall facedown before God and give up our individual agendas for the greater good of the kingdom, that all may come to the saving knowledge of Jesus Christ. Walking in unity is key to the Gospel being preached effectively throughout the earth.

## BEING ONE

*There is one body, and one Spirit, even as ye are called in one hope of your calling;*
*One Lord, one faith, one baptism,*
*One God and Father of all, who is above all, and through all, and in you all.*

EPHESIANS 4:4-6

I have a problem with people who say that their church is eight years old and it is *the* church. Their view and perception of the body of Christ is much too limited, narrow, and misinformed. The Church is not just one local church body. It is not one denomination. It is not even all the believers in one generation. The Church is, was, and is to come. The bride of Christ is as eternal as Christ Himself. The whole Church — the saints which are, the saints which were, and the saints which will be — are one Church espoused to one Lord.

Along these same lines, Paul says there is one Spirit. Now, why does he say something that is so obvious? He must have visited our churches today! How many times have we endured the tongue-lashing of a believer who is supposedly speaking by the Spirit but is actually releasing personal frustrations or pent-up anger resulting from unresolved woundings and offenses? Then there is the believer who desires attention and uses the gifts to get it, touting their special revelation from "the Spirit" in our midst. This does nothing but cause confusion and erode the confidence believers have concerning the validity and work of the Holy Spirit, which destroys unity.

Now, I don't want to get off in a ditch here! Every word spoken in the congregation does not have to be perfect. When well-meaning but unlearned believers step out in faith and courage to give what the Holy Spirit is saying, we must encourage them and correct them when necessary. This is how they grow and develop their gift. What we must always remember, however, is that when the Holy Spirit speaks through a vessel, *He will never contradict the Word of God or Himself.*

The truth will be confirmed by the mouths of two or three, and all that is spoken will flow in a stream of edification and comfort. This is the "one Spirit" Paul is referring to. The Holy Spirit is not fragmented or schizophrenic. He is consistent and reliable, and what He says to one, He says to all. When He fills a room and speaks, He draws us to and lifts up Jesus. He unifies us in a powerful corporate anointing where yokes can be destroyed and the captives set free.

Then Ephesians 4:4 speaks of the hope of our calling. What is the hope of our calling? The resurrection! Paul takes us to the ultimate outward expression of unity — the resurrection — which, again, is supernaturally brought about by Jesus. Think about it: no believer who precedes us in death will go before us and those of us who remain will not lag behind. When Jesus comes for us, He will come for us *all.* In one split-second moment, we will all be caught up to meet Him in the sky!

> **O**ne Lord, one faith, one baptism,
> One God and Father of all, who is above all, and
> through all, and in you all.

EPHESIANS 4:5-6

There is *one* Lord who calls us, one faith that unites us, and we are all baptized into Christ when we are born again. Whatever our color, cultural background, race, doctrinal persuasion, or gender, there is one unifying force for us as believers and that is Jesus Christ. There are not two Gods — one for Jewish believers and one for Christian believers. God is not a black God or a white God, a Japanese God or a Hispanic God. He is one God, above all, in all, and through all.

If you are not baptized into Christ, these verses do not apply to you. The "all" to whom God is Father to in verse 6 is exclusively the body of Christ and not the world at large. The Church is the body of Christ, a living, breathing organism functioning under the direction of her Head, Jesus Christ. But no matter how you describe the Church, the most significant feature is her oneness. That we understand this point is a major concern of Paul's.

> For as the body is one, and hath many members, and all the members of that one body, being many, are one body: so also is Christ.
> For by one Spirit are we all baptized into one body, whether we be Jews or Gentiles, whether we be bond or free; and have been all made to drink into one Spirit.

1 CORINTHIANS 12:12-13

**79**

Oneness among believers is not plain or homogenous; it is a dynamic oneness. God has chosen to take different individuals and join them together to make one whole. As a picture, the Church is like a jigsaw puzzle. Each piece alone has a strange shape and can even sometimes appear to be distorted. However, each piece is cut to fit perfectly with another piece of the puzzle, and when all the pieces are joined together (fitly joined), then and only then can the powerful, life-changing picture be seen.

Some of the most wonderful stories about unity seem to be associated with times of war. The dividing forces of prejudice and bigotry seem to disappear in the heat of battle. If you are in a foxhole with a guy, you don't care what color his skin is. You care whether he's on your side or not. So it is with the kingdom of God and our warfare against the devil. We are on the same side as other Christian believers, and we have a common enemy, a common problem, a common conflict. If we are going to win the battles we face against Satan, we must come together.

Ultimately, we all have the same need to be forgiven by God and accepted into His Beloved. We all need the same divine medication for our souls: God's love. If I have a deadly disease it makes no difference to me whether the anointed one praying for me is yellow, red, black, or white. I will gladly allow them to lay their hands on me! If my heart is broken and I need restoration, it makes no difference to me that I didn't grow up in the same neighborhood as the one who is preaching the healing of old wounds and offenses from the past. I must be willing to say, "Your God is my God. I am trusting the God whom we both serve to deliver me and make me whole."

The gifts of the Holy Spirit are distributed by Him into the body of Christ through people from all walks of life with diverse kinds of talents and abilities. We need to recognize our own unique gifts and develop them as part of our walk in Christ Jesus, but we must never separate our gifts from the whole body. We must never see our administration or talent as being better than or apart from the Church as a whole. We have one God who gives each of us gifts, and He is the one who orchestrates how they will all fit together in a powerful whole.

Our walk truly becomes a power walk when we put away all our offenses and disagreements and come into the unity of the faith. We will never agree on every doctrine, but we can agree on the essentials. Jesus is our Lord and the Head of the body of Christ in which we are members. Through the Holy Spirit who lives within each of our hearts, we become one.

When we walk in unity with one another, our walk puts the unity achieved at the tower of Babel to shame! Those who were building that miraculous structure at Babel were commended by God for their achievement of unity. However, their agenda was a selfish, self-serving one which was of no use to His kingdom. Thus, God was justified and even compelled to confuse them and thus destroy that powerful unity.

However, when God's mandate is being carried out by joyful spirits in the Church who are in love with Him and each other, the Bible says that nothing will be withheld from them. There is no issue of confusion to be reckoned with, because God's will is the only consideration of His body. As this occurs, the Church will literally tear down the gates of hell and establish righteousness, peace, and joy on this earth.

# 5

## WALKING IN THE SPIRIT

*Grieve not the Holy Spirit of God, whereby ye are sealed unto the day of redemption.*

EPHESIANS 4:30

Paul is literally *commanding* us to stop grieving the Holy Spirit, so it must be of paramount importance to him and to us. The word "grieve" means to outrage and humiliate, as a king who has been deposed by his subjects. Even though it is not possible to depose Jesus Christ, we are still capable of dethroning Him from our hearts and turning our passion and zeal toward people or things that have come to distract us from God's will and truth.

Grieving the Holy Spirit is to say and do things that He must turn His back upon, things which prohibit Him from participating in our lives to the full extent He desires. The chief cause of grief to the Holy Spirit is walking in the lusts of the flesh. When we walk in the flesh, doing what we want to do, when we want to do it, and the way we want to do it, apart from God's truth and commandments, the Holy Spirit simply says, "I can't go there. I can't be a party to that. I can't help with that. I can't participate." We shut off the Spirit's function in our lives when we choose to sin and to engage in behaviors that are contrary to God's purposes.

Now, this does not mean that the Holy Spirit leaves us. Paul is very clear on that point. He says in verse 30, "Ye are sealed unto the day of redemption." When we believe in and receive Jesus as our Savior, the Holy Spirit moves into our lives and seals us. He infills us and He resides within us until the day of redemption — which is the day we enter God's direct presence in eternity.

*For he hath said, I will never leave thee, nor forsake thee.*
HEBREWS 13:5

The Holy Spirit never leaves us or forsakes us. He seals us unto the day of redemption. The words "sealed" and "redemption" present the very essence of what Jesus did for all believers. "Seal" means "to mark as a means of identification." This kind of mark denotes ownership and carries with it the protection of the owner.

"Redemption" has a narrow and specific definition. It means "to pay the price for, to buy back from, to take ownership of by paying the ransom price." This word picture is awesome. Paul is showing us our state of being before salvation, when we were held captive by a cruel master. But then Jesus came and redeemed us, paying the price for our release from the enemy and all the bondage in which he held us. We then became Jesus' property, and He seals us or marks us as His. We are sealed by the Holy Spirit as a sign to all that we enjoy the protection of Jesus.

Therefore, because we are sealed unto the day of redemption by the Holy Spirit, we are able to walk in this world and not become a part of it. We are able to walk and not be destroyed by the destroyer. We are sealed, marked, secured, and protected. We have been bought with a price, freeing us from Satan's grip and setting us securely in the arms of Jesus, able now to serve our Lord and Savior with gladness.

However, when we choose to follow the dictates of our own fleshly desires, we disconnect ourselves from the Holy Spirit's favor in our lives. He cannot manifest Himself in anything that is contrary to the will and goodness of God. He will not act to help us to sin or to do anything that is contrary to God's nature, purposes, and commandments.

The Holy Spirit will not help you to lie or avoid the consequences of doing so. He will manifest

Himself only as you tell the truth, confess your lies, and obtain forgiveness from them.

The Holy Spirit will not help you to cheat another person, neither will He help you avoid the consequences for getting caught when you cheat. However, the Holy Spirit will manifest Himself when you seek to treat others honestly and make restitution to those you have cheated.

The Holy Spirit will not help you to seduce another person's spouse, neither will He help you cover up that seduction or that act of adultery. However, the Holy Spirit will manifest Himself in helping you to resist the temptation to sin and to terminate an illicit love affair. He will help you to live in sexual purity.

The Holy Spirit desires to be on our side! He delights in helping us — in giving us the information and discernment we need, in leading us into right decisions and right actions, in giving us the inspiration and motivation to act righteously and courageously, and in strengthening us to withstand evil and to speak and act in truth. The Holy Spirit wants to see us grow in Christ Jesus, move toward perfection, resist the devil, manifest His fruit, and operate in His gifts.

When we choose to act against God's desires and to do things our own way, the Holy Spirit is grieved. Paul says, "Don't do it!"

## SIX THINGS THAT GRIEVE
## THE HOLY SPIRIT

*Let all bitterness, and wrath, and anger, and clamour, and evil speaking, be put away from you, with all malice.*

EPHESIANS 4:31

Paul identifies six things that he knows with certainty always bring grief to the Holy Spirit:

- bitterness
- wrath
- anger
- clamor
- evil speaking
- malice

Look at this list closely. Most of these things can be held internally for a fairly long period of time without others knowing what is going on inside. Eventually, however, what is festering inside us is going to erupt and the pus of these vile wounds will make us offensive to the Holy Spirit and those we are sent to serve. The best way to grieve the Holy Spirit and destroy unity is to operate in these six things; the way to please Him and preserve unity is to avoid these six things at all personal cost.

**Bitterness.** A person can live with bitterness for years, but eventually that bitterness is going to leak out. It is going to manifest itself as acid remarks that corrode relationships, weaken the mettle of our peace, and ultimately cause depression or even illness. More insidiously, it is going to manifest itself in unforgiveness. And when we choose not to forgive others, we limit the forgiveness of God toward us. Jesus said, "Forgive, and ye shall be forgiven" (Luke 6:37).

The Holy Spirit loves to reveal Himself as God's mercy and love in an atmosphere of forgiveness. When we forgive, the cancer of bitterness cannot take hold of our soul and the Holy Spirit is free to flood our lives with the blessings of God.

**Wrath.** Wrath is rooted in a spirit of revenge — it is a strong desire to get even, to destroy one's enemy, and in the process to advance one's own personal power and position. A person can plot revenge for years and never act on it. What eventually happens is that they become so consumed with revenge that they no longer have the time or inclination to think about ways of advancing the Gospel or of speaking the name of Jesus to bring healing to another person. The person who is consumed with revenge cannot witness to the person they desire to see destroyed.

"Oh," some say, "I'm leaving vengeance up to the Lord." And in the next breath, they are whispering, "I just wish God would hurry up and cut their head off!" That's a spirit of wrath at work. Any time you desire something bad to happen to another person rather than to see that person come to experience the fullness of God's forgiveness and mercy in their life, you are captivated and obsessed with wrath.

The Holy Spirit flows through people who have yielded themselves to Him in love and overcome their desire to be vindicated. They have chosen to see people experience God's healing balm instead of His painful judgment.

**Anger.** Anger is actually rooted in a desire for power, being denied something that we want or which we think we deserve. When we feel this acute sense of losing control over a situation, we lash out and become abusive. One of the things we have to understand about abuse is that those who abuse are not acting out of hatred. They are acting out of a desire to show or to regain power. They are reacting to someone's put-down, rejection, or refusal to be controlled. Anger is saying, "I'm going to get mine," "I deserve more," "I'm not being treated fairly," "I'm not being shown the dignity and respect I deserve."

Some expressions of anger are not sinful, such as righteous indignation, a zeal for the things of God when they are maligned, and a disdain for satanic victories over families and governments. When anger at injustice, unrighteousness, and evil is turned toward acts of ministry and giving, it becomes the hot fuel for the flame of the Holy Spirit to work miracles of deliverance.

However, most anger is rooted in selfishness and it is dangerous for us to justify it or rationalize it. When we do this, we are deceiving ourselves and "do not the truth," because in reality we are serving our selfish lust for power. (See 1 John 1:6.) If we allow anger to fester in us, eventually it will manifest in an unrighteous, unholy way. We will lash and gash and crash, rather than seek out a solution that is strong and effective and righteous. When anger boils over, it burns and destroys.

Anger can reside in a person long before it manifests itself, and all the while, it will grieve the Holy Spirit and thus hold us back. While we are grasping and striving for personal power and control over any or all areas of our lives, we are cutting off the power of God to work in and through us.

The Holy Spirit is waiting for the body of Christ to empty themselves of all personal lust for power so that He can fill us to overflowing with God's power. Then we can do mighty exploits for the kingdom in Jesus' name.

**Clamor.** To clamor is to make noise or to shout in a way that is disruptive. Clamor is rooted in a general restlessness because something is perceived to be missing or lacking. A person clamors to be heard when he feels left out or unnoticed. They clamor for more when they feel cheated, short-changed, or deprived. Inside them, clamor is a feeling of being frustrated and dissatisfied.

Have you ever met a person who just couldn't be satisfied or was never at peace with themselves? There are people who always seem to be stirring up the pot, bringing up past hurts, nagging for more, or agitating for something else — it might not even be something better, just something different.

To clamor is the opposite of "to be content." Paul wrote to the Philippians, "I have learned, in whatsoever state I am, therewith to be content" (Philippians 4:11). That doesn't mean that Paul was content with the status quo at all times. Rather, he had learned — he had trained himself, he had acquired wisdom and understanding — to have a content and peaceful spirit regardless of outward circumstances.

Ultimately, putting off clamor is a matter of trust. The person with a *clamoring* spirit is a person who hasn't fully learned to trust God to provide, protect, or to act according to what is best for them and every person involved with their life. The person with a *contented* spirit is a person who trusts God to provide, protect, and act in a way that brings the greatest blessing and the greatest eternal reward.

> *Though I speak with the tongues of men and of angels, and have not charity [love], I am become as sounding brass, or a tinkling cymbal.*
>
> 1 CORINTHIANS 13:1

Sounding brass, tinkling cymbals — a noisy clamor! The person with a clamoring spirit is a person who is not truly loving. The clamoring person is always wanting more for *self.* To clamor is to say, "Pay more attention to me, give more to me." The loving person is one who accepts what God gives with thanksgiving and praise, and who seeks to give generously to others.

A person with this kind of agitated, discontented, unloving spirit of clamor can keep that feeling hidden for only so long, but eventually it will show itself. The Holy Spirit cannot work in a person who continually calls attention to self rather than to Jesus Christ. To clamor is an act of pride, and God will not share His glory with a proud person. However, the Holy Spirit will move mountains for the humble spirit who is content in all situations and trusts God implicitly regardless of the circumstances.

**Evil Speaking.** Evil speaking is translated from the Greek word *blasphemia,* which literally means "to injure another's good name, to slander, or to utter a defamatory statement or report." We may explode, lashing out at others close to us and even at those we love deeply. Or we may seethe, always on the verge of saying something we know we'll regret, always trying to hold ourselves in. Whether thinking it or actually saying it, evil speaking is evil and will destroy our lives.

Eventually, evil speaking will keep a believer from thinking the thoughts of Christ Jesus and witnessing the love of Jesus. The renewal of our mind is going to be thwarted every time we speak evil of someone else, and we will fail to grow spiritually. The Holy Spirit, on the other hand, loves to speak His words of edification and comfort through a person who has put away all evil speaking and, therefore, the law of kindness is always on their tongue.

**Malice.** To have malice is to be motivated by hatred. It is the ultimate in moral inferiority and decay because it is the exact opposite of love. Malice can be directed toward one individual, a group of people, or to a type of person. Malice is at the root of disharmony and a lack of unity. It is what gives rise to prejudice, bigotry, and many forms of retaliation, hurtful words, and harmful deeds.

Malice is a close associate of each of the other things Paul says grieve the Holy Spirit, because it is simple hatred. Hatred and bitterness go together. Hatred and wrath are companions. Hatred and anger are often linked. Hatred and clamor work hand in hand. Hatred and evil speaking are brothers.

Malice is at the other end of the spectrum from love and brotherly affection. It is contrary to the very nature of the Holy Spirit. The Holy Spirit cannot manifest Himself where hatred exists, because the foremost fruit of the Holy Spirit is love.

In summation, when the Holy Spirit is grieved by any one or a combination of these six things, not only is the individual believer's life destroyed, but unity in the body of Christ is seriously disturbed or totally destroyed. Therefore, it is essential for us as believers to guard our hearts and minds and avoid at all cost the entanglements of these things.

Does the Holy Spirit create, nurture, produce, or cause bitterness? Absolutely not. The work of the Holy Spirit is mercy.

Does the Holy Spirit generate wrath and vengeance in a person? Never. The work of the Holy Spirit is reconciliation and unity.

Does the Holy Spirit inspire anger from a loss of personal power and pride? Not at any time. The work of the Holy Spirit is to help us yield to the will of God and to praise God humbly in all things.

Does the Holy Spirit bring about clamoring in us? No. The work of the Holy Spirit is to give us peace and joy.

Does the Holy Spirit initiate or encourage evil speaking? No. The work of the Holy Spirit is forgiveness, blessing, and edification.

Malice and all of the other attitudes and behaviors that grieve the Holy Spirit grieve Him because they are totally opposite to His nature and the work He desires to do. "Don't do these things," says Paul.

## KINDNESS AND TENDERNESS

*Be ye kind one to another, tenderhearted, forgiving one another, even as God for Christ's sake hath forgiven you.*

EPHESIANS 4:32

What is it that Paul says we *are* to do? In our terminology today, Paul says, "Just be nice to one another."

We all know what it means to be tenderhearted. Just think for a moment of a mother who lovingly cradles and rocks her child, kissing him and holding him close and singing softly to him. Now, that child may have just fallen in the mud, been in a fight with another child, or won a prize at school that day. It makes no difference to the tenderhearted mother. She loves that child and cares for that child with just as much tenderness. Any error the child may have made, and any correction that may have been taught, has absolutely no bearing on the amount of tenderness the mother feels or expresses. This is her child! God feels the same way about His children, and it is His supreme desire that we are as tenderhearted to one another as He is to each of us.

We all know what it means to be kind. Just think for a moment of the person who gently and generously helps another person who is in need, sickness, sorrow, or any kind of trouble. The cup of water to the thirsty person. The meal to the homeless man. The warm shawl to the homeless woman. The visit to the lonely person in the nursing home or to the prisoner in the county jail. The kind person offers no condemnation to anyone for being thirsty, homeless, old, sick, or in jail. There's only respect, affirmation, and genuine concern. Again, this is how God treats us and how He desires us to treat one another.

What is done in tenderness and kindness is done quietly, simply, and genuinely. It isn't intended for show. It is intended as an expression of selfless love.

"Be tenderhearted and kind," says Paul.

"But," you may say, "I don't feel tenderhearted toward all people." Ask God to help you change the way you feel. And until you feel tenderhearted, act tenderhearted anyway! Paul does not say to *feel* tenderhearted. He says to *be* tenderhearted. The more you *act* tenderhearted — the more you *do* tenderhearted things to others and for others — the more you are going to start feeling tenderhearted!

You may not know what to say to the person who is grieving in the funeral home. Just go and sit quietly with them. That's *being* tenderhearted.

You may not know what to say to the person who is sick in the hospital. Just go and say a prayer for their healing in the name of Jesus. That's *being* tenderhearted.

You may not know what to say to the person who is scared about a doctor's appointment. Just go with that person and hold their hand while they sit in the waiting room. That's *being* tenderhearted.

The more you perform kind and tenderhearted acts, the more you are going to find your heart opening up to others and the more you will desire to show tenderness. The same goes for kindness. We all know the kind thing to do for a person in need. Do that kind thing! You may not *feel* kind, but Paul didn't say anything about feeling kind. He said, *"Be* kind." Pick up that person who needs a ride to church. Hold that crying baby while that mother deals with her crying toddler. Secretly leave a sack of groceries on the back porch steps of the family you know is going through a hard time. Call and give a word of encouragement to the person you know has just been fired from a job. *Be* kind.

If you have any doubt about what the kind or tenderhearted thing may be, ask the Lord to reveal it to you. The Holy Spirit will probably remind you of something Jesus did. Any time you have a question about what to say or how to act, look to Jesus. Do what He did.

Jesus preached good news to the meek.

He bound up the brokenhearted.

He proclaimed liberty to the captives.

He opened the doors of the prison to those who were bound.

He proclaimed what was acceptable to the Lord.

He comforted those who were mourning.

He replaced ashes with beauty.

He substituted sadness with joy.

He removed a spirit of heaviness and adorned them with a garment of praise. (See Isaiah 61:1-3.)

The Holy Spirit is always pleased whenever we act like Jesus!

## FORGIVENESS

**B**e *kind and compassionate to one another, forgiving one another, just as in Christ God forgave you.*
EPHESIANS 4:32 NIV

When we truly begin to see others as God sees us — people who are in need of forgiveness, transformation, renewing of their minds, mercy, and God's grace — we cannot help but forgive others and show kindness and tenderness toward them. It is only when we think that somehow we *deserve* the forgiveness of God that we feel we have the right to look down on others and deny them the same grace by which we are forgiven.

The fact is, none of us deserves the goodness of God! None of us are worthy of God's love and mercy. None of us could claim salvation on our own merits. We each are saved because God first loved us, sent His Son to die for our sins, and chose to indwell us with His Spirit. The only way any person ever got into the true Church is by way of forgiveness.

If God had not forgiven you, you would have no relationship with Him. You would not have the promise and hope of eternal life. You would not have the Holy Spirit residing in you. You would not know what it means to lay down guilt and shame and move into a new life of purity and wholeness. All people — including you — are in need of forgiveness, and it is when we keep that fact clearly in mind that we are going to find it much easier to resist the things that grieve the Holy Spirit and, instead, to be kind and tenderhearted toward others.

Jesus taught His disciples:

> Forgive us our debts, as we forgive our debtors.
> If ye forgive men their trespasses, your heavenly Father will also forgive you:
> But if ye forgive not men their trespasses, neither will your Father forgive your trespasses.
>
> MATTHEW 6:14-15

It doesn't get any plainer than that!

To be forgiven is to be set free of guilt, shame, and recrimination. It is also to be set free to love others and to do good to them. When we forgive others, we are not saying that sin doesn't matter. Sin is deadly and it is a deadly serious issue to God. God never winks at sin. But to forgive others is to say, "I am not going to heap guilt, shame, and recrimination on you. I am not your judge or your jury. I free you so God and God alone can deal with you. I set you free in *my heart* and in *my mind*."

To receive forgiveness from God is to take the same approach: "I receive God's forgiveness for my past. I am not going to hang on to guilt, shame, and recrimination. I am not going to remind myself continually of what I once was or once did. I am going to free my mind to think about those things that God desires for me to think about!"

Some believers I know haven't forgiven their own children for doing things that aren't half as bad as things they once did. Forgive your children! Don't continue to lay guilt and shame on them. As long as you take on the role of judge and jury for your child, you are not going to be able to be free to do what it is God truly wants you to do with and for your children. Furthermore, you will self-destruct and short-circuit the power of God in your own life.

Some believers have not forgiven their parents. Even if you were abandoned, your parents divorced, or you were abused by them, forgive your parents. Refuse to continue to place blame on them. Free them from your judgment. As long as you are holding resentment and bitterness against them, you cannot receive the joy of the Lord in your own heart or be used by God to set others free.

Whatever we do not forgive, we are destined to repeat. That's a truth I wish I could hammer into your heart. If you do not forgive that abusive parent, you will repeat the pattern of abuse in your life. It is inevitable. If you do not forgive that person who hurt you in a past relationship, you will strike out at every person who comes into relationship with you. You will not be free to love and to be loved.

Your past is tied to you through the umbilical cord of unforgiveness. When you forgive, you cut the cord. But if you do not forgive, you continue to be tied to that sin or that hurt and you will repeat it. That's the way curses are passed from generation to generation. Something is held on to that should have been forgiven, cleansed, changed, or let go.

Our Christian experience begins with repentance and forgiveness but is sustained by continually purifying our hearts and our motives. Maturity is reached as we submit ourselves to a lifestyle of obtaining forgiveness from God and those we have offended and then by turning around and granting forgiveness to those who have offended us. When we live according to the law of forgiveness, our hearts remain pure and tender, our spirits are light, our minds are free, our vision is clear, and our manner and speech will be kind — filled with the power of the Holy Spirit to save, heal, deliver, and set free.

Forgiveness — from God for ourselves, toward others, and toward ourselves — is the key to avoiding and conquering any temptation to fall into the things which grieve the Holy Spirit. We then, being free from all spiritual hindrances, are unified in our purpose and position and empowered by the Spirit to conquer the enemy, possess our promised land, and glorify our Savior.

## WALKING IN LOVE

**B**e ye therefore followers of God, as dear children;
And walk in love, as Christ also hath loved us, and
hath given himself for us an offering and a sacrifice to
God for a sweetsmelling savour.

EPHESIANS 5:1-2

Have you ever seen a little boy strut about a room just like his daddy? He swaggers and holds his head and swings his arms just like his father — and he doesn't even know he's walking like him. And what about the little girl who walks just like her mama walks? She tilts her head and puts her hand on her hip just like her mother. She hasn't decided to do that, she has just copied that way of walking without even thinking about it. She is an exact copy and a precise duplicate of her mama.

Paul wrote to the Ephesians, "Walk like your Father. You are His child, so walk like Him." As believers in Jesus Christ, we are God's children, and that is an overwhelmingly awesome concept to any human being. We are born of His Spirit, which means that spiritually speaking, we are His direct offspring in every spiritual sense of the word. Paul is exhorting us to grab this truth and live it by imitating the Father who gave birth to us. But how do we attempt this? Paul gives us the answer in the following verse, when he exhorts us to walk in love in the same way that Jesus also loved us.

We are to walk, talk, think, and behave just like Jesus. Now, if Paul had written to the Ephesians, "Walk in love," it would not have been nearly as challenging as what he actually says: "Walk in love, *as Christ also hath loved us.*" Our challenge is not to love in our own ability to love, but to love *as Christ loves.* There is a vivid example of this concept in 2 Corinthians:

> **B**lessed be God, even the Father of our Lord Jesus Christ, the Father of mercies, and the God of all comfort;
> Who comforteth us in all our tribulation, that we may be able to comfort them which are in any trouble, by the comfort wherewith we ourselves are comforted of God.

> 2 CORINTHIANS 1:3-4

Paul reminds us how Jesus comforted, delivered, and encouraged us and how He continues to do so whenever we go through a difficult and even tragic time. He instructs us to minister to and help each other in the same way Jesus ministers to and helps us.

Remember how you were blessed by that special word from the Lord, the one He impressed on your heart just at the moment when you were about to lose hope? Do you recall the enormous relief that flooded your soul when you expected a rebuke for your flawed behavior, but instead He encouraged you and strengthened you to stand strong, ready to overcome at the next temptation.

If we just think about how much His kindness, grace, mercy, and love meant to us then and mean to us today, we can understand what kind of effect being kind, gracious, merciful, and loving will mean to someone else who is going through a trial. Believers who extend grace and compassion are imitating Jesus every bit as much as those who seek to raise the dead and multiply two fish and five loaves of bread into a feast for five thousand. Jesus' ministry on earth was marked by spectacular displays of power as well as spectacular displays of love.

Forgiving the woman caught in adultery, sending her home redeemed and restored, is also a hallmark of Jesus' work on earth. If we are going to be just like Him, we must find people who are hurting, abused, and even wrong and minister to them until they become healed, restored, and right. Ultimately, our walk is going to be a walk that is the very manifestation of love.

*This is the message that ye heard from the beginning, that we should love one another...*

*We know that we have passed from death unto life, because we love the brethren. . . .*

*My little children, let us not love in word, neither in tongue; but in deed and in truth.*

1 JOHN 3:11,14,18

It was John who said that the very nature of God is love. All that He does is motivated by love, grounded in love, and displayed in love. (See 1 John 4:8.) John 3:16 tells us that God loved mankind so much, He gave His only begotten Son to die for our sins and provide the way back to God. The motivation for God's every act was and is love. Therefore, we are to walk in the high calling of Jesus' love for others. Our challenge is to walk through every day in such a way that we reflect the love walk of Jesus.

If you want to walk as a Christian, imitate Christ. Any time you wonder what the loving thing is to do, look at what Jesus did. Love people the way Jesus loved people and the way He loves you.

## SACRIFICE OF SELF

*And walk in love, as Christ also hath loved us, and hath given himself for us an offering and a sacrifice to God for a sweetsmelling savour.*

EPHESIANS 5:2

Paul calls Jesus' love "a sacrificial offering." One of the definitions of "sacrifice" is "victim" and the word "offering" could be rendered "presentation." Jesus allowed Himself to be presented as a victim on our behalf. See Him at Calvary, being mauled and tortured for evil, despicable thoughts and acts which He never experienced. He accepts our guilt and pays the price for it just so God can love us and be loved by us without restraint. His is a sacrifice born of a desire to bring the love of God to a lost and dying world and restore to the Father His lost children. Jesus went to extraordinary lengths, well beyond what was necessary, to insure us access to God.

Paul says that the sacrifices we make in love are a "sweetsmelling savour" to God — they are like wonderful aromatic incense rising up to Him. God delights in our expressions of love to other people. We give Him pleasure through our acts of genuine Christlike love. But it isn't easy to love like that! Paul doesn't make any claim that such love is easy or automatic. He calls such love a sacrifice — it is something we must choose to do willfully and consistently, and it goes against our fleshly nature. We have to *choose* to empty ourselves on behalf of others. We have to *choose* to die to self so we can love others more generously.

We have a tendency to think that some people are just more loving than others, that some are just a "natural" at showing love or doing the loving thing. That isn't the Bible truth. The Bible says that love is always a choice and that it is a choice that costs us something. It costs us our pride, our worldly reputation, and our preoccupation with self. No person can be loving toward others while staring into a mirror. No person can give to others while clutching his wealth in his hands in fear. To genuinely love, we have to put ourselves aside — and that is painful. It goes against our nature of desiring to be number one. Genuine love is always in some form of self-denial, because we are putting someone else — their care, interests, and well-being — before ourselves.

Many people I know are waiting for the love of God to envelop them to the point where they become some sort of floating divine being who walks around and does wonderful loving things for others. That isn't the way it works! There are no prepackaged Christians. There is no "add and stir" formula for God's love to gush forth.

To be loving, we must choose to nail our will to the cross. We must choose to die to our own selfish desires and ambitions. We must choose to make loving others our priority, a priority that is right next to that of loving God. Jesus declared believers subject to two great commands, which are like an umbrella over all of God's other commands:

*Thou shalt love the Lord thy God with all thy heart, and with all thy soul, and with all thy mind.*
*This is the first and great commandment.*
*And the second is like unto it, Thou shalt love thy neighbour as thyself.*
*On these two commandments hang all the law and the prophets.*

MATTHEW 22:37-40

Our walk — everything we say, everything we do, and everything we are — is to be a reflection of our love for God and our love for others.

## LOVE IN ACTION

*But fornication, and all uncleanness, or covetousness, let it not be once named among you, as becometh saints;*
*Neither filthiness, nor foolish talking, nor jesting, which are not convenient; but rather giving of thanks.*

EPHESIANS 5:3-4

Walking in love and holiness is not automatic with conversion. Our spirits are converted from old creature to new creature, but our actions are still subject to our will and are the outcome of choices we make. Nobody is immediately or instantly moral because they accept Jesus as Savior. Immoral acts of the past are forgiven, but salvation is not an *automatic* vaccination against all immoral acts in the future.

All Christians, and especially new ones, must pray to God for the guidance of the Holy Spirit in everything they think, say, and do. At the same time, they must seek to have their minds renewed by the Word of God. Otherwise, it is possible for them to give their hearts to Jesus and continue to smoke and drink and curse and chew and run around with those who do — and not even see any line of distinction between what is right and wrong in these areas! Without the enlightenment and discipline that comes from God's Word and the Holy Spirit, no believer can be trained to godly behaviors, of which love is the highest.

In Ephesians 5:3-4, Paul is making it very clear to us that sexual immorality, uncleanness, and covetousness are *not* acts that can co-exist with the love of God. For example, those who practice fornication are users. They are out for their own pleasure, seeking only to use another person sexually, without any thought to God's command-ments or love for that person. This is the exact opposite of what Jesus would do.

Those who are "unclean" are into perversion, a vicious immorality that flaunts itself in the face of God's love and commands. Being unclean is a blatant rejection of all that is holy and pure and righteous. Where fornication is simply sexual activity outside of the law of marriage, uncleanness is practicing every extreme and deviant unnatural behavior. Examples of uncleanness would be everything from rape to bestiality to sadistic and masochistic acts.

Those who covet are manipulators. They are always trying to see how they can get what someone else has. To covet is to be on the *take*. That is the exact opposite of the way Jesus acted. Jesus was always on the *give*.

Paul also speaks about filthiness. Ephesus was a city in which there were lots of orgies that were related to the false goddess Diana. Hallucinogenic drugs and excessive drinking were a part of those ungodly feasts connected to the Temple of Diana. Have you ever seen the aftermath of a party of drunks or drug users? The result is filth. There's nothing of Jesus Christ associated with filth.

Finally, Paul condemns foolishness and jesting, which are the exact opposite of being sober-minded. Being sober-minded is holding those things which are important to God, those things which are dear and precious to Him, as dear and precious to us. Foolishness and jesting are making light of the things that are important to God, teasing about things that are eternal, and joking about God and the work of God in people's lives. This is a very dangerous practice, and certainly reveals no great love for God or His people.

> **T**his ye know, that no whoremonger, nor unclean person, nor covetous man, who is an idolater, hath any inheritance in the kingdom of Christ and of God.
>
> EPHESIANS 5:5

The truths Paul is conveying to the Ephesians in this passage of Scripture are foundational truths about character, morality, and personal discipline, truths which are essential to the Christian love walk. However, Paul is also giving a highly sober warning to the believer: Do not practice these things or you will not receive your inheritance in the kingdom.

When we love God and respect and love others, we will not fornicate or perform unclean acts. We will not covet or fall into filthiness or foolish thinking and behaviors, because our life belongs to Jesus Christ. As a result, God can open the windows of blessing in our lives and pour out our inheritance. Peter describes our inheritance most succinctly:

> **H**is divine power hath given unto us all things that pertain unto life and godliness.
>
> 2 PETER 1:3

When we choose to walk in love, all the power of God backs us up and goes into action to pour

His abundant life into ours. We triumphantly and humbly experience our inheritance in Christ — prosperity of every kind — spirit, soul, and body. The *result* of love in action is moral and selfless behavior, but the *reward* of love in action is the manifestation of our inheritance in the kingdom.

## A THANKFUL HEART

Paul puts one main thing on the ledger sheet opposite fornication, uncleanness, covetousness, filthiness, and foolishness and jesting: giving of thanks. Thanksgiving is the beginning of our praise and worship. It is also the beginning of morality and forgiveness.

When you are truly thankful for another person's life before the Lord, you won't want to engage in fornication with that person.

When you are truly thankful for what the Lord has given to you and what the Lord has given to others, you won't covet what others have.

When you are truly thankful for your own salvation from sin and for the freedom God gives you not to sin, you won't want to engage in sin.

When you are truly thankful for the goodness and blessings of God, you won't want to engage in filthy behavior.

When you are truly thankful for your eternal life and for your salvation from eternal death, you won't want to make light of God's mercy and forgiveness.

The loving person is first and foremost a thankful person. They are a person who knows, "We love him, because he first loved us" (1 John 4:19). If God had not loved us first and reached out to us in His mercy and love, we could not have become His children. If He had not sent His Son, Jesus, to die on the cross, we could not have been spared the consequence of spiritual death for our sinful nature. Love flows freely from a thankful heart!

## LOVE IN THE CHURCH

Making a commitment to walk in love sounds very noble and grand when we declare it, but walking it out is another matter, and Paul knew that firsthand! The fact was, the church in Ephesus was a mixed bag. There were mature believers and brand-new believers. Some needed to be taught and some needed to be reminded of what they had been taught already. We're no different today.

Some of the believers in the Church today have come out of lifestyles that were just as bad as anything found in Ephesus — orgies, drugs, incest, idolatry, and prostitution. Other believers have followed the traditions of the Church all their lives and they are so uptight about the rules and rituals that they have totally overlooked the joy of salvation and what it means to be led by the Spirit.

A man said to me one day, "What is the anointing? You keep talking about the anointing and I don't know what you mean."

I was a little surprised at his ignorance and said, "You don't?"

He said, "No, I came to Jesus out of the Nation of Islam. In all my life, I never heard that term 'anointing.'"

Despite my busy schedule, the time had come for me to do a little teaching...and to do it in love. All that we do — to all who are on the walk with us as believers and unbelievers to whom we witness — must be done with love. We must sacrifice ourselves to serve and help and give just as Jesus did and continues to do for us.

Variety and differences are part of the challenge of our walk in love. We are called by God to love all kinds of people from all walks of life and at all levels of maturity. We aren't given the privilege of walking only with people who are just like us. Some of the people who are walking with us know things we need to learn. Others need to be taught, discipled, and trained by us and our example. We are to love all people: those who are over us in authority and lead us by their example; those who are, spiritually speaking, brand-new, crying babies in dirty diapers; and those who are seeking, striving, and determined to overcome their weaknesses and please their heavenly Father — just like we are.

> **A** *new commandment I give unto you, That ye love one another; as I have loved you, that ye also love one another.*
> *By this shall all men know that ye are my disciples, if ye have love one to another.*
>
> JOHN 13:34-35

Jesus said that the world would know the Church by the love we have for one another, and that love is a supernatural, heavenly love that comes straight from the heart of God.

> **T**he love of God is shed abroad in our hearts by the Holy Ghost which is given unto us.
>
> ROMANS 5:5

Walking in love is a miraculous and divine way of life which can only be realized as we yield ourselves fully to the Holy Spirit, completely abandon our selfish concerns, and obey Jesus' command to love with every fiber of our being. If every member of the body of Christ would follow Jesus' words in John 13:34-35, not only would the Church be transformed and transcend the power and potency of the early Church, but it would once again turn the world upside down!

*Let no man deceive you with vain words: for because of these things cometh the wrath of God upon the children of disobedience.*

*Be not ye therefore partakers with them.*

EPHESIANS 5:6-7

Paul was aware that there were men roaming about the various churches of his time teaching that certain types of sin and disobedience were either acceptable or didn't matter to God. This was a Greek way of thinking, for many of the Greeks held to the opinion that they could do anything they wanted in their bodies because the body didn't really matter, only the spirit mattered. This was not the wisdom of God!

*Know ye not that ye are the temple of God, and that the Spirit of God dwelleth in you?*

*If any man defile the temple of God, him shall God destroy; for the temple of God is holy, which temple ye are.*

*Let no man deceive himself. If any man among you seemeth to be wise in this world, let him become a fool, that he may be wise.*

*For the wisdom of this world is foolishness with God.*

1 CORINTHIANS 3:16-19

Paul stood 100 percent against that teaching and warned us that judgment comes on those who choose to continue in fleshly sins once they know better. We are to avoid such behavior and to avoid people who believe such behavior is acceptable. We are not to listen to man's wisdom, which is foolishness to God. We are to walk in God's wisdom. He goes on to remind us:

*Ye were sometimes darkness, but now are ye light in the Lord: walk as children of light:*

*(For the fruit of the Spirit is in all goodness and righteousness and truth);*

*Proving what is acceptable unto the Lord.*

EPHESIANS 5:8-10

If you have questions about what is good and right before God, ask a mature believer. Study what the Bible says and pray for revelation from the Holy Spirit. Seek godly counsel. If you have any doubt whatsoever about whether you are acting in a wise manner that will bring a sweet aroma to God's nostrils, search for an answer from godly sources and do not act until you have complete peace.

## BE THE LIGHT!

To have the Light of the World within you and then to choose to walk in darkness is to utterly obliterate your witness for Jesus Christ. When you choose to sin or act upon man's wisdom, you deny the Holy Spirit any opportunity to work through you. If you need a standard, Paul says to look to what is good, right, and true. The Holy Spirit will always produce fruit that is marked by goodness, righteousness, and truthfulness. Anything else is not of Him.

Paul doesn't leave it at that. He doesn't just say, "Don't sin." He goes a step further and says, "Don't associate with those who do sin. Speak out against their sin." Those are strong words.

> **H**ave no fellowship with the unfruitful works of darkness, but rather reprove them.
> For it is a shame even to speak of those things which are done of them in secret.
> But all things that are reproved are made manifest by the light: for whatsoever doth make manifest is light.
>
> EPHESIANS 5:11-13

Does this mean we are never to be around sinners? No. The fact is, you must be around sinners to have the opportunity to share the Gospel of Jesus Christ and to lead an unbeliever to salvation. What Paul says is that we are not to have "fellowship with the

121

unfruitful works of darkness." We are to avoid sinning. We are not to seek out, go along with, party with, or associate routinely with the sinful activities of unbelievers. We are to have absolutely no ties with sin.

Furthermore, we are not to dismiss sin or to attempt to justify it, either in ourselves or in others. We are to *reprove* sin. We are to stand against it, speak against it, and in the face of sin, do the very opposite — display the love and righteousness of God.

Finally, we are not even to speak about works of darkness. When we speak about something, we intensify it, call attention to it, diminish its shame, and can even glamorize it. That's one of the major flaws in our world today. Sin seems to be discussed and paraded about in movies, on talk shows, and depicted in every prime-time program on television. The more sin is talked about, the less shameful it becomes. Children grow up thinking, "Everybody does this. Everybody talks about it. There's nothing wrong with something everybody talks about and everybody does."

Nothing could be farther from God's truth!

When we put sin on center stage, we are giving it permission to become familiar. We are giving permission for others to study it, gawk at it, become accustomed to it, and eventually to say, "It's all right."

That's why Paul strongly admonishes us not to talk about the shameful things done in spiritual darkness. Instead, he tells us to choose to be innocent of those things and be the light. Any time darkness comes our way, we should shine even brighter!

When someone comes around to tell you a dirty joke, say, "I'd rather not hear that. May I tell you about the love of God instead?" If they persist in their effort, walk away. When someone comes around to try to entice you into having sex with them, say, "I don't do that. Will you go to church with me instead?" If they persist, walk away.

There's no good fruit from sin. That's why the works of darkness are called *unfruitful*. Sin has consequences that are deadly, and those consequences are not fruit. Fruit is pleasant, good, nourishing, and life-giving. Although sin is pleasurable for a season, in the end it always produces the exact opposite. It is unpleasant, evil, depleting, and life-destroying.

> **A**wake thou that sleepest, and arise from the dead, and Christ shall give thee light.
>
> EPHESIANS 5:14

For some of the Ephesians and for many believers today, these words of Paul are a literal wake-up call. Paul knew that many were just aimlessly walking along, so tied up in worldly things and sin that you would never know by looking at them that they were believers. Paul could not have made this plainer: If you are born again but persist in the works of darkness, you will be asleep among dead people. Although you are spiritually alive, you have repressed and suppressed your spiritual life and light by your acts of disobedience and are nothing more than a reflection of the darkness in which you are walking. If you put a sleeping person in a room of dead people, you would have to get very close to the one sleeping to tell they were alive.

If that is you, WAKE UP! Look where you are going. Open your spiritual eyes. You are about to sleepwalk right over a cliff! Move far away from sin and those who encourage you or entice you into sin right now. If you do this, the Word of God promises that Jesus will give you light, and that is the wisdom of God. From this moment on, if you have any doubt about what is right, ask Jesus. He'll show you what is right. He'll guide you into the truth of what is pure, holy, and righteous before God. Be the light!

In reality, the only way to be the light and walk in the light is to walk with wisdom Himself. The Bible says that Jesus is wisdom to us. (See 1 Corinthians 1:30.) He is the Living Word. (See John 1:1,14.) When we walk with Jesus, have fellowship with Him, seek His counsel at all times, and love Him and worship Him as we go about our day, we will walk in the light and grow in the light.

> **T**his then is the message which we have heard of him, and declare unto you, that God is light, and in him is no darkness at all.
> If we say that we have fellowship with him, and walk in darkness, we lie, and do not the truth:
> But if we walk in the light, as he is in the light, we have fellowship one with another, and the blood of Jesus Christ his Son cleanseth us from all sin.
>
> 1 JOHN 1:5-7

It is very simple: When we walk in the light, we will be the light!

## THE PRINCIPAL THING

> **W**isdom is the principal thing; therefore get wisdom: and with all thy getting get understanding.
> Exalt her, and she shall promote thee: she shall bring thee to honour, when thou dost embrace her.
> She shall give to thine head an ornament of grace: a crown of glory shall she deliver to thee.
>
> PROVERBS 4:7-9

When Solomon became king of Israel, he was just a young man, but God told him He would give him anything he wanted. Talk about the brass ring! What would you do if Jesus appeared to you today and said, "I'll give you anything you desire. Just name it, and it is yours right now"? But Solomon did not ask for the fastest chariot in the world, the most beautiful wife in the land, or even the wealth of all kingdoms. This incredible young man asked God for wisdom.

As a result of his request, God granted Solomon wisdom and everything that comes with wisdom: riches, wealth, and honor such as no other king had possessed or ever would possess after him. (See 2 Chronicles 1:7-12.) Every blessing in life rested upon the foundation of wisdom. Therefore, it is not surprising that Paul sums up the walk of the believer by writing to the Ephesians:

> **S**ee then that ye walk circumspectly, not as fools, but as wise.
>
> EPHESIANS 5:15

The word "circumspectly" is a very interesting word in the Greek. It depicts perfection in the sense of being exact, careful, and accurate, and it leaves no room for any quality or characteristic of life that is undisciplined, untrained, unholy, ungodly, or unrighteous. To walk circumspectly, we must be entirely focused on what *God* is desiring to accomplish in us, through us, for us, and around us. We must be exact, careful, and accurate, making certain that our lives — our thoughts, our speech, our actions, and our motives — line up perfectly with God's Word and the guidance of the Holy

Spirit at all times. A circumspect walk is a walk in which we pay attention and "take heed" to ourselves.

The message here is that our wandering stage in sin and distraction from God's will is over. It's time to cross over the Jordan River and enter into the fullness of what God has promised us, our inheritance as His children and believers in Jesus Christ. If we truly are going to walk in victory, claiming every bit of territory that the devil seeks to possess in our lives, we are going to have to walk focused squarely upon the truth of God, shunning anything that would lead us astray or make us veer from the path God has set for us.

> **R**edeeming the time, because the days are evil.
>
> EPHESIANS 5:16

There's no delay in this! No more wasting time in foolish thinking, ungodly fantasy, and carnal appetites. No more justifying delay. It's time for us to know our calling, our purpose, our hope, and the will of God — and march into the promised land to take all He has promised!

> **W**herefore be ye not unwise, but understanding what the will of the Lord is.
>
> EPHESIANS 5:17

Wisdom is always intimately connected with understanding. When we walk in God's wisdom, we have His understanding of a situation. We may not know all the details or even see the outcome in the beginning, but we have a deep sense of God's eternal plan and purpose in every action He directs us to take. Inevitably, as we walk out God's plan, He enlightens us with understanding and we see how each piece of the puzzle fits perfectly. Zodhiates states that understanding is the ability to "put something together and make sense of it," and in the experience of the believer, it is a divine, eternal, all-knowing sense that emanates from God Himself. Understanding is something believers have the privilege to walk in while the world around us stumbles in darkness, ignorance, and confusion. That's why people in the world greet each other with, "What's going on? What's happening?" They don't know! They are without understanding.

Paul does not leave us out there, wondering how in the world we are to get wisdom and walk in understanding in our practical, everyday lives. He goes on to give us very specific instructions.

> **A**nd be not drunk with wine, wherein is excess; but be filled with the Spirit;
> Speaking to yourselves in psalms and hymns and spiritual songs, singing and making melody in your heart to the Lord.
>
> EPHESIANS 5:18-19

There has been a lot of controversy in the Church concerning the consumption of alcoholic beverages, but I believe that is almost a distraction and a tangent from the message God is bringing to us in these verses of Scripture. The point is that we are to be filled with the Spirit. Nothing else in life should satisfy, motivate, or drive us but being filled with the Spirit. Not only is being filled with the Spirit the only way we will be able to walk in the wisdom of God's Word and will, but it is the only way we will have a magnificent, awesome, and joyful experience in doing so!

In order to be filled with the Spirit, however, we must *speak to ourselves*, and we must speak the right things: psalms, hymns, and spiritual songs. We must make melody in our hearts, praising and worshipping our Lord at all times. This is God's simple prescription for a healthy, happy, fulfilling, and successful Christian walk, and yet we spend most of our time doing something else.

How many people do you know who are consumed by their work?

How many people spend every spare minute on a hobby or pastime that is of little consequence?

How many people do you know who are wasting precious time reading or watching things that are of absolutely no eternal benefit, which actually draw them away from the things of God and pull them down?

How many people do you know who spend every weekend at the lake, in the mountains, at the beach, or any place other than the house of God?

Paul says to us, "Don't let anything consume your time, attention, or energy but the Spirit!"

There is nothing wrong with working, resting, playing, and growing, and certainly the Word of God encourages us to do these things. However, the great thing about being filled with the Spirit is that you can be filled with the Spirit wherever you are and whatever you are doing. You may not be able to sing psalms, hymns, and spiritual songs while you are working, but you can make melody to the Lord in your heart! There is no activity in which we cannot at least have a heart filled with praise and worship to God.

How is all this really connected to wisdom? When you have a heart filled with the Spirit, making melody unto the Lord, you are plugged into wisdom Himself. You are connected to the Divine Revelator of Truth and the Power of the Universe. You are walking hand in hand with Jesus, the King of Kings and Lord of Lords, who is the Alpha and the Omega and knows the end from the beginning.

The surest way to know whether you are in God's will and walking in His wisdom and understanding is whether or not you are making melody to Him in your heart. If you feel uncomfortable doing that or are not doing it, something is wrong and you are heading for the cliff like someone who is asleep among the dead! But the good news is that in one moment of time you can be right back on track by simply repenting, turning your heart back to God, and beginning to sing psalms, hymns, and spiritual songs to Him.

Wisdom is the principal thing because it is the key to everything good, holy, and worthwhile in life. By being filled with the Spirit and walking in God's Word, we will not only accomplish the call of God on our life, but we will experience marvelous adventures and great blessings along the way!

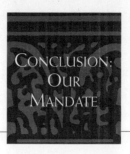

## CONCLUSION:
## OUR
## MANDATE

*I*n the book of Ephesians, God gives the Church the mandate to cross the Jordan and take the land. There's no justification for refusing to walk forward in the fullness of His promises. To choose to continue wandering in the wilderness, staying in sin, delaying our growth, avoiding our call, denying who we really are, and focusing on things other than the Word and the Spirit is to choose death. That is not our walk or our mandate from God. We are to be the light, expel the darkness, and bring prosperity and peace to the hearts of mankind. When the hearts of men are filled with the prosperity and peace that come through knowing Jesus Christ as Lord and Savior, every aspect of their lives becomes beautiful and fruitful.

But to achieve our mandate from God, we must walk His way. Our walk is to be a responsible walk, always giving honor and glory to the One who saved us, healed us, and set us free by staying on the path He has designed for us. We are to walk as the new creature we are in Christ, showing forth His character and compassion to everyone we meet. Our walk is a walk of supernatural strength, continuously relying on our Father God's ability and not our own to exceed and shatter all expectations for our lives. Our walk is not alone, but hand in hand with Jesus and with each other, in unity and in love, which gives us our potency and power to reach and transform the world. And finally, our walk is a wise walk, based not on our human, foolish ideas and perceptions, but on the very mind and heart of God which is revealed to us by His Word and His Spirit.

Our walk is powerful, and it brings results and rewards which reach far beyond our own little sphere of influence — in this life and the life to come.

# REFERENCES

*Adam Clarke Commentary.* 6 vols. Adam Clarke. *PC Study Bible.* Version 2.1J. CD-ROM. Seattle: Biblesoft, 1993-1998.

*Barnes' Notes on the OT & NT.* 14 vols. Albert Barnes. *PC Study Bible.* Version 2.1J. CD-ROM. Seattle: Biblesoft, 1993-1998.

*The Bible Knowledge Commentary: An Exposition of the Scriptures.* Dallas Seminary faculty. Editors, John F. Walvoord, Roy B. Zuck. Wheaton, IL: Victor Books. 1983-1985. Published in electronic form by Logos Research Systems Inc., 1996.

*Brown, Driver, & Briggs' Definitions.* Francis Brown, D.D., D. Litt., S. R. Driver, D.D., D. Litt., and Charles A. Briggs, D.D., D. Litt. *PC Study Bible.* Version 2.1J. CD-ROM. Seattle: Biblesoft, 1993-1998.

*Expositor's Bible Commentary, New Testament.* Frank E. Gaebelein, General Editor. J. D. Douglas, Associate Editor. Grand Rapids, MI: Zondervan Publishing House, 1976-1992.

*A Greek-English Lexicon of the New Testament and Other Early Christian Literature.* Walter Bauer. Second edition, revised and augmented by F. W. Gingrich, Fredrick Danker from Walter Bauer's fifth edition. Chicago and London: The University of Chicago Press, 1958.

*The Greek New Testament.* Editor Kurt Aland, et al. CD-ROM of the 3rd edition, corrected. Federal Republic of Germany: United Bible Societies, 1983. Published in electronic form by Logos Research Systems, Inc. 1996.

*Greek (UBS) text and Hebrew (BHS) text.* PC Study Bible. Version 2.1J. CD-ROM. Seattle: Biblesoft, 1993-1998.

*The Hebrew-Greek Key Study Bible.* Compiled and edited by Spiros Zodhiates, Th.D. World Bible Publishers, Inc., 1984, 1991.

*Interlinear Bible. PC Study Bible.* Version 2.1J. CD-ROM Seattle: Biblesoft, 1993-1998.

*Jamieson, Fausset & Brown Commentary.* 6 vols. Robert Jamieson, A. R. Fausset, and David Brown. *PC Study Bible.* Version 2.1J. CD-ROM. Seattle: Biblesoft, 1993-1998.

*A Manual Grammar of the Greek New Testament.* H. E. Dana, Th.D. and Julius R. Mantey. Toronto, Canada: MacMillan Publishing Company, 1927.

*Matthew Henry's Commentary.* 6 vols. Matthew Henry. *PC Study Bible.* Version 2.1J. CD-ROM. Seattle: Biblesoft, 1993-1998.

*The New Linguistic and Exegetical Key to the Greek New Testament.* Fritz Reineker, Revised version by Cleon Rogers and Cleon Rogers III. Grand Rapids, MI: Zondervan Publishing Company, 1998.

*Strong's Exhaustive Concordance of the Bible.* J. B. Strong. *PC Study Bible.* Version 2.1J. CD-ROM. Seattle: Biblesoft, 1993-1998.

*Vincent's Word Studies in the NT.* 4 vols. Marvin R. Vincent, D.D. *PC Study Bible.* Version 2.1J. CD-ROM. Seattle: Biblesoft, 1993-1998.

*Wuest's Word Studies from the Greek New Testament for the English Reader.* Volume One, Ephesians. Kenneth S. Wuest. Grand Rapids, MI: Wm. B. Eerdmans Publishing Company, 1953.

**T. D. Jakes** is the founder and senior pastor of The Potter's House church in Dallas, Texas. A highly celebrated author with several bestselling books to his credit, he frequently ministers in massive crusades and conferences across the nation. His weekly television broadcast is viewed nationally in millions of homes. Bishop Jakes lives in Dallas with his wife, Serita, and their five children.

To contact T. D. Jakes, write:
T. D. Jakes Ministries
International Communications Center
P. O. Box 210887
Dallas, Texas 75211

or visit his Web site at:
*www.tdjakes.org*

# Books by T.D. Jakes

### Six Pillars From Ephesians

*Loved by God* • *Experiencing Jesus*
*Intimacy With God* • *Life Overflowing*
*Celebrating Marriage* • *Overcoming the Enemy*

*Lay Aside the Weight*
*Lay Aside the Weight Workbook & Journal*
*Loose That Man & Let Him Go!*
*Devotions from Loose That Man & Let Him Go!*
*Loose That Man & Let Him Go! With Workbook*
*So You Call Yourself a Man?*
*T. D. Jakes Speaks to Men!*
*T. D. Jakes Speaks to Women!*
*Woman, Thou Art Loosed!*
*Woman, Thou Art Loosed! Devotional*

# Videos by T.D. Jakes

*The Insights on Ephesians Series* (Six Videos)
*Rock for the Thirsty Soul*
*Praise in the Midst of Pain*
*Overcoming Your Limitations*
*Talk Your Way Out*

# BECOME THE MAN
# ❖GOD❖
# WANTS YOU TO BE!

Bishop T.D. Jakes' message of hope, healing, and freedom in the name of Jesus has changed countless lives. In his lasting bestseller *Loose that Man and Let Him Go!* Bishop Jakes offers clarity, restoration, and healing to a generation of men—both believers and seekers—confused about their purpose, vision, and role in today's culture. He urges men to let Jesus take hold of their limitations, put away all excuses, step forward, and become all that He intends for them.

Newly updated, the book also includes a workbook that will help you apply everything you learn.

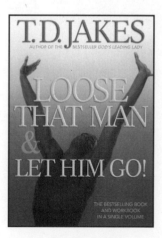

*Loose That Man & Let Him Go!*
by T. D. Jakes

BETHANYHOUSE